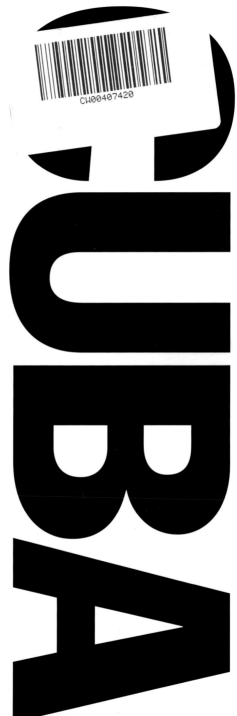

SPIRAL GUIDE

CUBA

CW00407420

AA
Publishing

Contents

STOP PRESS

At the time of printing the Cuban government has elected to eliminate the US dollar from circulation in Cuba and US dollars are no longer accepted to purchase goods or services. This will affect the currency information in this book. Check the current situation before travelling.

Written by Andrew Forbes

Copy edited by David Henley
Verified by Colin Hinshelwood
Indexed by Andrew Forbes
Page design by Douglas E. Morton
CPA Media, Chiang Mai, Thailand

Published by AA Publishing, a trading name of Automobile Association
Developments Limited, whose registered office is Southwood East,
Apollo Rise, Farnborough, Hampshire, GU14 0JW. Registered number
1878835.

ISBN 10: 0-7495-4362-0
ISBN 13: 978-0-7495-4362-4

All rights reserved. No part of this publication may be reproduced,
stored in a retrieval system, or transmitted in any form or by any
means – electronic, photocopying, recording or otherwise – unless the
written permission of the publishers has been obtained beforehand.
This book may not be sold, resold, hired out or otherwise disposed of
by way of trade in any form of binding or cover other than that in which
it is published, without the prior consent of the publisher.

The contents of this publication are believed correct at the time of
printing. Nevertheless, AA Publishing accept no responsibility for any
errors or omissions or for changes in the details given in this guide or
for the consequences of readers' reliance on this information. This does
not affect your statutory rights. Assessments of attractions, hotels,
restaurants and so forth are based on the author's own experience and
contain subjective opinions that may not reflect the publishers' opinion
or a reader's experience. We have tried to ensure accuracy, but things do
change so please let us know if you have any comments or corrections.

A CIP catalogue record for this book is available from the
British Library.

© Automobile Association Developments Limited 2005
Maps © CPA Media 2005

Cover design and binding style by permission of AA Publishing

Colour separation by Leo Reprographics
Printed and bound in China by Leo Paper Products

Find out more about AA Publishing and the wide range of services the
AA provides by visiting our website at www.theAA.com

A01753

the magazine

Where RHYTHM Rules

Cuba is universally renowned for its pervasive, complex musical rhythms. It doesn't seem to matter whether it's rain or shine (though the latter doubtless helps) – a street party, a fiesta, a religious ceremony, a bar, night club or even a funeral – the music never stops.

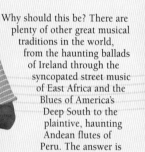

Why should this be? There are plenty of other great musical traditions in the world, from the haunting ballads of Ireland through the syncopated street music of East Africa and the Blues of America's Deep South to the plaintive, haunting Andean flutes of Peru. The answer is probably quite simple – a compulsive fusion of two of the world's truly great musical traditions blended and set against a backdrop which – colonial servitude or socialist austerity regardless – remains essentially warm, rich and welcoming.

At the very heart of Cuban musical tradition lie the complex percussive rhythms of West and Central Africa. The most important of these is probably that of the Yoruba people (▶ 16), one of the three great tribes of modern Nigeria. To this has been added the sophisticated music of Spain, based on traditions that are as much Berber and Arab as they are Castilian and Basque. Add a touch of French musical tradition – especially from around Cienfuegos (▶ 102) where many refugees from the 1791 Slave

Left:
Saxophonist in Santiago de Cuba
Above:
Everybody dances
Previous page:
Street artists in La Habana Vieja

Rebellion in Haiti settled – plus a natural flood of joy, lively celebration of femininity and virtual surfeit of machismo, and you have the roots, at least, of Cuba's unique, vibrant and inescapable musical tradition.

Most contemporary music in Cuba is based on *son*, a form of Latino "country music" believed to have originated in the east of the country in the 19th century. Over the intervening years it has grown more and more sophisticated, with instruments such as horns, flutes and fiddles added to the original combination of guitar, bongo, double bass and – central to just about all Cuban music and creating a rhythm it's just impossible to ignore – the *claves*, two ridged sticks rubbed or beaten together to mark the beat.

By the 1940s son had given rise to more complex, larger sounds such as *rumba*, *mambo* and *cha-cha-chá*. In the mid-20th century

Cuban music blends the percussive rhythms of Africa and Spain

Girls dancing at an impromptu street party in La Habana Vieja

(and not entirely unrelated to the growing emigrant community in the Unites States following Castro's 1959 revolution), *salsa* emerged as a universally popular musical form of expression across North America and beyond. Meanwhile, an unexpected but very positive input to Cuban music was made in the 1980s by Castro's lengthy military interventions on behalf of the socialist regimes in Ethiopia and Angola – a form of cross-cultural fertilisation.

Cuban music is generally joyful, and folks really do dance in the streets – not just young people moving apparently effortlessly (and often sensually)

**Above: Varadero cabaret
Right: Street guitarist in Santa Clara**

at street-side parties, but older people waltzing happily in the many parks that distinguish most Cuban cities. Cubans – long driven to exasperation by the capricious economic policies of their government – like to say that music, dancing and making love are the main activities, beyond government control, which make life tolerable!

One way for the visitor to Cuba to experience this extraordinary musical experience (other than just walking the streets) is to visit a *casa de la trova* (House of Troubadours), found in most – if not all – Cuban cities. Here musicians sing and play everything from *sol* to *salsa* to traditional *trova* (ballads) all day and much of the night. Cubans love – adore – their music, and will go to endless lengths to explain and encourage the complex yet driving rhythms to enthusiastic outsiders.

Perhaps the best known song in Cuba is *Guajira Guantánamera*, (Farm Girl of Guantánamo), composed in the 1920s by Joseito Fernández. The words added to this romantic and enduringly popular song were taken from the *Versos Sencillos* of the father of the nation, José Martí. The song is so popular it's become a virtual second national anthem.

Rastafarian at Havana street party

If Cuba is famous for two products other than the ubiquitous sugar which blankets most of the island, they are…

rum and Cigars

Rum is a direct product (though certainly not the only one) of the island's endless sugar fields and tall, smoke-belching sugar mills. To produce rum – or *ron* as it is known in Cuba – local distilleries take the highest quality molasses or *miel de cana* (cane honey) and dilute it with water, adding yeast and allowing the subsequent mix to ferment for around 30 hours. The fermented brew is then heated before being allowed to condense in a copper vat. Generally the resultant liquor is tested and either strengthened or weakened until it is around 75 per cent proof.

The young rum is then stored in oak barrels and allowed to mature for three, five or even seven years. Various ingredients from caramel to baby guavas may be added to produce different flavours. The result is quite a drink, and distinctively Cuban – at least when served in such famous cocktails as the *daiquirí* (a blend of rum, lemon juice, sugar, maraschino and crushed iced, shaken rather than stirred) or the *Cuba Libre* (rum, cola and crushed ice, stirred rather than shaken).

Fine Cuban cigars and a selection of Cuban rums

The list is long. Havana Club, the country's largest producer and supplier of rum, provides a list of over 100 "Cuban Classic Cocktails" for those with a yen for rum, a bar of their own, or just a lot of time on their hands!

The Cuban Revolution of 1959 did away with perhaps the most famous of the island's labels – Bacardí Rum was first distilled in Santiago de Cuba in 1878, but following Castro's seizure of power departed for nearby Puerto Rico in 1960. The factory remains, however, still in Santiago, now producing the well-known Caney brand. Also in Santiago is the **Museo Emilio Bacardí Moreau** (▶ 136), founded in 1899 and one of the oldest rum museums anywhere in the world. Finally visitors should not miss the highly elaborate art nouveau **Edificio Bacardí** building just east of Havana's Parque Central – and only a short walk from Ernest Hemingway's old watering holes of **El Floridita** and **La Bodeguita del Medio** (▶ 67) – what better place for a tall, iced rum cocktail?

Above: Bar sign in La Habana Vieja
Below: Sugar mill at Australia, Matanzas Province

Cigars are another matter. Everyone agrees that Cuba produces the best in the world, but not everyone agrees that they're good for your health – though the same could, of course, be said of too much rum! The best cigar tobacco is said to come from **Pinar del Río** (▶ 78) in the west of the island, and especially from **Vuelta Abajo** (▶ 87).

Top: Tobacco leaves drying, Vuelta Abajo
Inset: Making cigars, Pinar del Río

For decades names such as Cohiba, Montecristo and Romeo y Julieta have been celebrated world-wide, not least for the fondness of the rich, famous and powerful to smoke them. Examples that spring readily to mind are Winston Churchill, Groucho Marx and John F. Kennedy – the latter is reliably reported to have ordered 1,200 of the very best Cuban cigars from an aide in Washington the day *before* he signed the anti-Cuban embargo bill! Yet another famous cigar smoker is – or perhaps was – Fidel Castro himself. According to the Cuban authorities Fidel gave up smoking in the mid-1980s, commenting "they're good for the country, but not for my health". Not everyone believes in this conversion, though – a cigar worker in Pinar del Río simply sneered at the prospect, commenting (but very discreetly): "Oh Castro – now he smokes in the toilet!"

Cigars remain big business for Cuba (even without the American market), and around 100 million are exported annually, earning the island an estimated US$50 million a year. The best place to observe the tobacco harvest and cigar manufacturing process is in Pinar del Río and nearby Vuelta Abajo – but be aware that stories of young Cuban women rolling the tobacco leaves on their thighs is just another urban myth. Alternatively, if Pinar del Río seems too distant, visitors can also witness the production process and make purchases from the restored and extremely elegant **Partagás Factory** to the west of Central Havana's Parque Central (▶ 60).

Like most nations – only perhaps more so, considering a good deal of the original indigenous culture was
lost to the ferocious, gold-seeking, god-preaching
Conquistadors – much of Cuba's history is buried
forever in its deep past.

ORIGINS

of a

NATION

*A*rchaeologists believe that the first human beings may
have reached Cuba as long ago as 3500 BC, although car-
bon-dated remains have only been found as far back as 2000
BC. These earliest settlers were Amerindian people known as
the Guanahatabey, who settled mainly in the west of the
island, and the Siboney, who occupied the east. As far as we
can tell, they lived mainly by fishing and hunting. It was not
until around AD 1000 that they were joined by the
more numerous Taino people, refugee agricultur-
alists from the nearby island of Hispaniola.

All this was to change on 28 October,
1492, when the ships of the navigator
Christopher Columbus first made landfall at Gibara on the northeast coast.
Columbus decided the island was part
of Asia, and declared it "the most beautiful land human eyes have ever seen".
Following a circumnavigation of the
island in 1508 this was proved to be a
serious misconception; it was left to
the explorer Hernando Cortez to cross
the Isthmus of Panama and stare "with
a wild surmise" on the Pacific almost
30 years later.

This didn't stop the Spaniards
returning to Cuba in 1512, when an
expedition led by Dieqo de Velázquez –
Cuba's first governor – landed at
Baracoa and began the island's long
colonial servitude. The bust of one
of the first independence martyrs, the Indian chief Hatuey,
still stands outside the
church at Baracoa
where he was
burned
alive

by the Spanish invaders.

But Cuba was to prove a disappointment to the early Conquistadors. There simply wasn't much gold to be found, the local Amerindians died in droves from disease and overwork, and even religious conversions went badly – Hatuey declined to be baptised before his execution on the (entirely reasonable) grounds that "he didn't want to see another Spaniard again, even in heaven"!

Cuba did serve the Conquistadors in another way – as a source of fresh meat and food, as well as a safe haven for the ongoing enterprise of conquering Mexico and Peru. Following the decimation of the native Indians, the Spanish turned increasingly to African slaves as a source of labour. The first were brought as early as the mid-16th century. Over the next two centuries Cuba developed as a vital source of cattle, tobacco and sugarcane.

Baracoa's Cruz de la Parra

Not that Spain's supremacy in the Caribbean would remain unchallenged for long. Other European nations – the French, Dutch and most notably the British – turned up seeking a slice of the pie, occupying outlying islands where they set up as pirates, freebooters and buccaneers (not for nothing is Cuba's most popular beer today called Bucanero!)

Perhaps the most important development for Spanish colonial authority in the New World occurred in 1783 when the United States won its independence from Great Britain. A superpower was in the process of developing, and Cuba – indeed all Latin America – had a new and mighty neighbour to the north.

Between 1810 and 1825, under the guidance of the great statesman and liberator Simón Bolívar, all mainland South America won its independence from Spain, leaving only "loyal Cuba" as Spain's major colonial possession in the region. Part of the reason for this loyalty was Spanish fear of the African slaves who now dominated much of the country. In 1791 a slave revolt in neighbouring Haiti resulted in

Plaque at the former home of Simón Bolívar

Bust of the Indian resistance leader Hatuey in the main square at Baracoa

Spanish prisoners of war are taken from Havana to Key West, Florida 1898

the overthrow of French power and the flight of thousands of white settlers, terrifying many Cuban Whites whose slogan became "better a Spanish Cuba than a Black Cuba". Meanwhile the US continued to cast covetous eyes on the rich island. In 1848 Washington offered Madrid US$100 million to buy Cuba outright, raising the offer in 1854 to US$130 million. The Spanish foreign minister refused, declaring he would "rather see Cuba sink beneath the waves". But the writing was already on the wall, and the days of Spanish dominion were numbered.

In 1868 Spain's high-handed attitude and general colonial arrogance sparked the long-delayed revolt. It started in the traditionally rebellious east of the island, about as far from Spanish-influenced Havana as possible. Among the numerous Cuban independence fighters who emerged from the resulting Wars of Independence, two stand head-and-shoulders above the rest.

The first of these was Carlos Manuel de Céspedes (1819–78), regarded by all Cubans as the first national hero of their independence. On 10 October, 1868, he rang the great bell on his sugar estate at La Demajagua, near Manzanillo, announcing the simultaneous freedom of his slaves and Cuba's declaration

José Martí

of independence from Spain. Ten years later he was shot dead by Spanish soldiers.

The second and greatest of all Cuban national heroes was the independence leader José Martí (1853-95). In 1881, to escape the Spanish, Martí went into exile in New York where – after some initial exuberance at the relative personal freedom – he learned to recognise "the entrails of the monster (the USA) he was living in". He returned to Cuba in 1895, but was killed without firing a single shot during his first skirmish with the Spanish occupiers. Nevertheless today there is a bust of Martí, "the sincere man from the land of the palm tree", in every town, village and hamlet in Cuba.

Soon after the American domination Martí had foreseen came to pass. In 1898, following the still unexplained sinking of the battleship *USS Maine* off Havana Harbour, the US declared war on Spain and quickly seized control not just of Cuba, but of Puerto Rico, Guam and the Philippines. Cuba became a protectorate by law, but a colony in all but name. By the mid-1920s US big business controlled the Cuban economy, while American gangsters and high-rollers used Havana as their personal, exotic playground.

In 1952 power was seized by a corrupt, pro-US army sergeant called Fulgencio Batista who proclaimed himself dictator and ran Cuba for his own profit and that of his US cronies.

In this way the stage for the Cuban Revolution was already set (▶ 20).

Castro addressing a crowd

Cuba is considered a Catholic country. The influence of Catholic Spain set the official backdrop for Cuba's social and religious framework. But is Cuba really a Catholic country? The answer, fascinatingly, is both yes and no.

SANTERIA

Santería or the "Cult of the Saints" has transformed Cuban Catholicism to an extent that it is now, probably, the main religion among Cubans. Its influence is pervasive at all levels of society. Certainly it's a power to be reckoned with, and its influence seems to be growing rather than diminishing.

Santería originated among the Yoruba people of Nigeria – the main source of slave labour imported during the colonial years to raise sugar cane and perform other back-breaking tasks in the Cuban countryside.

Like so many other facets of Cuban society, Santería is the product of two inextricably opposed and yet very similar traditions. The Spanish masters forbade slaves to practice their "heathen" religion, known as *Regla de Ocha*, a belief system which acknowledges numerous *orisha* or gods in a way not entirely dissimilar to the cannon of saints recognised by the Catholic Church.

In Santería, Olofi is the supreme god. But he is remote and unapproachable, at least in a direct fashion. Rather supplicants must approach him through lesser divinities, the *orisha*. Santería recognises hundreds of *orisha*, but some are more important than others, and many have become associated with Catholic saints, so that a new, mixed religion developed in Cuba.

Santería devotees are easily spotted by their white clothing

Above: Santería priest with image of goddess
Left: Santería altar displaying paraphernalia of an *orisha* cult

and elaborate necklaces. Music, dance, drumming and trance are ways of communicating with *orisha*. Because of the prohibition on African religions imposed by the Spanish, many *orisha* took on dual identity associated with Catholic saints. Thus the *orisha* Obtala is linked with Jesus Christ, while his wife, Odudua, is connected to the Virgin Mary. Chango, the Yoruba God of War, is identified with St. Barbara.

It's easy to understand why an enslaved people tried to conceal and preserve their indigenous beliefs. More fascinating is how the process worked both ways – with many white, Spanish Catholics adopting elements of Santería belief so that today followers of Santería probably outnumber orthodox Catholics in Cuba.

For the visitor, it's easy to witness the outward trappings of this Afro-Cuban religion. Santería women dance regularly in the Plaza des Armas in La Habana Vieja, while cigar-smoking Santería priestesses pose for photographs.

Yet the real essence of Santería remains mysterious – it's not easy for the casual visitor to witness authentic ceremonies, and it may take many months of patient enquiries and investigation to meet and talk with serious initiates.

Many Cubans believe that their political leaders, both past and present, have a relationship with *orisha*. Thus both Batista and, more surprisingly, Fidel Castro, are held by many Cubans to be followers of Santería.

the MAFIA
connection

Between the US "liberation" of Cuba from Spanish rule in 1898 and the overthrow of the Batista dictatorship in 1959, Cuba became a centre for US military, business and Mafia connections.

The seizure of the US base at Guantánamo Bay dates from these years, as does American corporate domination of Cuban sugar and tobacco. Despite the granting of independence in 1902, Cuba remained a US colony in all but name for the next six decades. Meanwhile the US Mafia took over Havana and made it their playground. This era will be familiar to any aficionado of Mario Puzo's *The Godfather*.

The height of Havana's reputation as a sin city came during the time of the US Prohibition in the 1920s. Cuba emerged as a centre not just of alcohol consumption, but also of prostitution and gambling. The Mob moved in big time, buying up hotels, establishing casinos, and building flashy houses in Havana.

The Mob set up shop

The heyday of the Mob in Havana came after 1938, when Fulgencio Batista first seized power.

Batista invited Meyer Lansky, the "Jewish Godfather", to take over the running of the casino and racetrack businesses. Gambling flourished. The mob made a fortune, and massive kickbacks were paid to Batista.

In December 1946, the biggest Mafia convention since the Depression was held in Havana. Nearly every Mafia family boss from the US attended the event. Meanwhile the Cuban peasants sweated and slaved for peanuts. But many Cubans, including a young law student called Fidel

Castro, knew what was going on and bitterly resented the exploitation of their country by mobsters.

Fidel plots his revenge

In 1952, Castro and a band of compatriots launched a doomed attack on the Moncada Barracks in Santiago de Cuba. A year later, when the young firebrand was serving time in prison, Batista appointed Lansky his "personal adviser on gambling reform".

Under Batista efforts were made to promote tax-free tourism. Almost every hotel had a casino, and so profitable did the business become that even educated Cubans like doctors and teachers gave up their jobs to become croupiers.

During these years Lansky deposited more than US$3,000,000 in Batista's personal bank accounts in Switzerland. The corrupt old dictator eventually got away safely and died in comfort in Spain during the 1970s.

With Batista's overthrow in 1959 all this was to change. Castro issued a warning to the mobsters, particularly Lansky, "not only will we prosecute gangsters", he thundered, "we will certainly shoot them". Lansky promptly fled to the Bahamas where he is said to have offered a bounty on Castro's head.

But then Lansky died in 1983, and despite numerous assassination plots Fidel remains very much alive!

Opposite: Meyer Lansky
Above: One of the Batista-eras' many casinos
Centre: The Hotel Nacional still dominates the Malecón skyline

the magazine **19**

Fidel Castro, Raul Castro and Che Guevara

Since 1959 strongman Fidel Castro has dominated Cuban politics, a position made more secure by the personality cult surrounding the charismatic but long dead Ernesto Che Guevara. Indeed, Fidel is now the longest-ruling leader in the Western world, and the irony is few believe he would still be there were it not for continuing and unyielding US opposition to his rule.

The third of seven children of an affluent sugar farmer, Fidel Castro Ruz was born in 1927 in Finca Las Manacas in Eastern Cuba. He attended Catholic and Jesuit schools before studying law at Havana University where, in the company of other like-minded young revolutionaries, he concluded the dictator Fulgencio Batista (➤ 15) must be overthrown by force.

Castro's first attempt was staged on 26 July, 1953, at the Moncada Barracks in Santiago de Cuba. It failed militarily due to the rebels being hugely outnumbered, but Castro's legendary rhetoric did not. "Convict me", he told his judges. "What does it matter? History will absolve me". After a period of imprisonment on the Isla de la Juventud he went into exile where he met the young Argentinean doctor Ernesto Guevara. Together with a band of similarly determined rebels they sailed for Cuba on the yacht *Granma* (➤ 53), arriving in the southeast of the island. This time, after a prolonged guerrilla struggle, they were victorious.

Statue of Ché Guevara at Santa Clara

LOS

BARBUDOS

In the idealistic spirit of the times, *Los Barbudos*, as these bearded warriors were called, soon became icons for a generation. But what were they really like? Guevara was the son of middle-class Argentinean parents. He gave up a career in medicine to spread revolution and anti-imperialism across the world. His well-known, handsome features helped inspire tremendous loyalty and love for him among his followers, and not a little admiration from women.

As a consequence a Guevara cult developed, especially after his death. Castro, who continues to represent Che as a model of selfless sacrifice, has carefully nurtured this. In fact Guevara was – no doubt he had to be – quite ruthless. It was Chairman Mao who wrote that "revolution isn't a tea party". It certainly wasn't in China, and nor was it in Cuba. In reality Guevara ordered many executions, even carrying out some personally.

Nevertheless, when Che was captured and executed in turn by Bolivian soldiers in 1967, his handsome features became the perfect – and continuing – icon for the Cuban Revolution. Today Castro retains all government powers, yet more like a firm headmaster than a member of Bush's "axis of evil". Meanwhile the saintly image of Che is everywhere to be seen, generally accompanied by his most famous maxim – "Always Onwards to Victory!"

Cubans are bitterly divided in their opinions of the two men. Just about everybody, apart from party members and very close associates, can see that the economic process championed by the revolution has completely failed. Cuba is in a far worse state of poverty than it should be, and this is in major part due to poor socialist economics. But then there's the US economic blockade to take into consideration, too – it seems unfairly disproportionate to Castro's "excesses", and many Cubans consider it both petty and vindictive. Besides, no real Cuban patriot – even if an exile living on Florida's Palm Beach – wants to see their lovely island become just another colonial adjunct of the United States.

In other words, there's real pride in some of the achievements of the Cuban Revolution, as well as genuine despair at its economic and social failures. Most Cubans will probably be happy to see Castro go – but they'll let the process arrive naturally.

Meanwhile *El Jefe Maximo* (The Big Chief) – as Castro is often styled – may have written his own epitaph better than he could have realised in an interview with his friend the Colombian author Gabriel Garcia Marquez. Asked by the latter what he'd really like to do with his time, Fidel replied: "Oh, hang around on some street corner". He may not have achieved this for himself, but for the great majority of his impoverished countrymen he's been most successful.

Examples of the "Che" cult: contemporary road hoarding and collected writings

Hemingway & Greene

Cuba is closely associated with two great Anglo writers, Ernest Hemingway and Graham Greene. Interestingly, it is the macho, hunting shooting and fishing Hemingway who seems to capture all the attention, while the more intellectual, sympathetic and, frankly, engaging Greene receives relatively little attention.

Ernest "Papa" Hemingway

For more than 20 years Hemingway made Havana and its immediate environs his home, drinking in well-known watering-holes such as El Floridita and La Bodeguita del Medio (➤ 67). He was a passionate deep-sea fisherman, hanging out at Cojímar (➤ 63) and sailing his luxurious yacht, *El Pilar*, up and down the Florida Straits looking for Marlin and (between 1941 and 1945) German submarines.

Some of Hemingway's most famous works were penned in Cuba, most notably The *Old Man and the Sea*. Initially he made his home at Hotel Ambos Mundos on Calle Obsipo (➤ 64) in La Habana Vieja, though later he bought a ranch, Finca La Vigía, where he lived with this third wife Martha Gelhorn. A difficult man, much given to drinking, fighting and other so called "manly" pursuits, he was nevertheless popular with most Cubans (including, apparently, Fidel Castro), and remains one of this nation's favourite Americans.

Above: Hemingway with Castro
Below: Hemingway's "Old Man of the Sea", Cojímar

Hemingway's attitude towards the Cuban Revolution remains unclear, with both pro- and anti-Castro factions claiming his support. In fact he seems to have welcomed the overthrow of the dictator Batista, describing the *Fidelistas* as "honest revolutionaries" in a letter to a friend, and commenting on the flight of Batista "There goes the son of a bitch!" On the other hand he seems to have been anxious that the US administration should not push Castro into the Soviet camp.

Hemingway left Cuba in 1960 – having been diagnosed with inoperable cancer – and committed suicide in his native Idaho a year later. He is only known to have had one conversation with Castro, and they discussed – deep sea fishing

Still, Hemingway remains an ex-post-facto hero of the Cuban leadership and a powerful pull for the tourist business. There's a well-established Hemingway Trail encompassing the Hotel Ambos Mundos (➤ 64), the two bars – El Floridita and La Bodeguita del Medio – already mentioned, the Hemingway Museum at Finca La Vigía, 10km south of central Havana (➤ 63), La Terrazza Restaurant at Cojimar (➤ 63), and the large Marina Hemingway to the west of Havana – which actually had nothing to do with the man, but was named as a tribute to him.

"Papa", as he is affectionately known, is indeed something of a literary and political hero – a not very "Quiet American" whose machismo certainly struck a cord with many Cubans.

Graham Greene

But what of Graham Greene, whose most famous (and arguably best) novel was called *The Quiet American*, set in Vietnam?

Greene was of a quite different character to Hemingway, more sophisticated and indeed more cynical. *Our Man in Havana*, Greene's percipient novel of life in Batista's Cuba, may also have cut a little close to the bone. It recounts how a

Graham Greene

Far left: The bar at La Bodeguita del Medio
Left: Alec Guinness as Wormold in *Our Man in Havana*
Below: Noel Coward as Hawthorne in *Our Man in Havana*

British secret service agent, Jim Wormold, invents the presence of weapons of mass destruction hidden in the Cuban countryside both to please his masters and to improve his own finances. The novel, though written in 1958 (just a year before Batista's overthrow) may have come uncomfortably close to the mark when Soviet nuclear missiles were discovered in Cuba in 1962. Be this as it may, Castro condoned the book (though he denied it adequately represented the evils of the Batista regime) and approved its filming in Cuba.

For his part, Greene had a judicious respect for Castro. "In all Castro's speeches there is a sense of a man thinking aloud. He explains his course of actions, he admits mistakes... one has the sense that he respects the intelligence of his audience". Greene was less enthusiastic about Hemingway, however. After visiting the latter's home at Finca La Vigía he felt moved to comment: "taxidermy everywhere. Buffalo heads, antlers, such carnage..."

Sporting **CUBANS**

For a country with a population of only 11 million people, Cuba certainly fights above its weight, at least as far as sports are concerned.

*L*ike Australia, which also has a small population, but a fearsome record of sporting achievement, Cuba has produced many world-class athletes and sporting heroes. Much of this great achievement has occurred since Fidel Castro banned professional sport in 1962. The Olympics, with its amateur charter, was the perfect stage for Cuban sporting might.

Cubans had made their mark at the Olympics prior to 1962. In 1904, at the St. Louis Olympics, a Cuban fencing team won every medal available apart from the sabre event. But it was post-1962 that saw the real rise of Cuban sporting prowess.

Boxers began to dominate the Olympics at all weights. Since 1972 no less than 27 gold medals have been won despite Cuba boycotting the games in 1984 and 1988.

Alberto Juantorena (left), Cuba's champion middle-distance runner

Right: Cubans excel at many sports including cycling

Probably the two best-known boxers to the outside world were both heavyweights. Teófilo Stevenson, a giant of a man, was champion in 1972, 1976 and 1980, and would undoubtedly have won again in 1984 if the Cubans had not pulled out of the event. Once the Cubans rejoined the Olympics in 1992 another heavyweight waded in. Felix Savon went on to become champion in 1992, 1996 and 2000. Famous US boxing promoter, Don King tried to coax him into becoming a professional, offering him a staggering US$10 million: Savon's reply, "What do I need $10 million for when I have 11 million Cubans behind me." Even at the 2000 Sydney Olympics Cuban boxers managed six medals, four of which were gold.

Athletics have also produced some highs, most famously at the 1976 Montreal Olympics where an unknown Cuban, Alberto Juantorena, ran away with gold medals in the 400m and 800m, an unprecedented feat. On his return to Havana, Juantorena spent the next 15 days cutting sugarcane; even sporting heroes are part of the revolutionary struggle. These days he's Cuba's deputy sports minister.

Women have had similar successes. Maria Colón won the javelin gold medal at the 1980 Moscow Olympics, the first non-European to win for almost 50 years.

Currently 12,000 physical education teachers are employed in Cuba's schools and colleges. Every primary school student takes a minimum of 2–3 hours PE a day, and it is compulsory for all students to continue with PE classes until their second year of university.

Cuban teams have also performed well at the Olympics. Baseball aficionados will argue that the Cuban Olympic team from Barcelona in 1992 and again in 1996 at Atlanta was perhaps the greatest baseball team of all time.

THE BEST OF
Cuba

Although tourism in Cuba remains relatively undeveloped, the island's attractions are among the best in the world. It's true that certain irritations remain, but things are fast improving. Set these against the following highlights and you'll soon realise how much Cuba has to offer.

Colonial Architecture

La Habana Vieja (➤ 54) is the grandest concentration of classical Hispanic architecture to be found anywhere in the New World, though much of it remains in need of repair. Today it's gradually being restored to its former grandeur, often with the help of UNESCO. In particular don't miss the **Plaza de la Catedral** (➤ 62) and the narrow complex of streets around **Calle Obispo** (➤ 61), historic sites with an atmosphere matching anything in the Caribbean.

Colonial
architecture
in Camagüey

Fishing

Cuba's finest waters for deep-sea fishing, including sailfish, swordfish, tuna, barracuda and shark are found along the northwest coast, where the Gulf Stream flows through the Straits of Florida. These waters, much loved by the great angler and sportsman Ernest Hemingway (➤ 23), include especially the Golfo de Guanahacabibes and the waters off **Cojímar** (➤ 63).

BEST

Music and Dance

Musicians at a restaurant in La Habana Vieja

All Cuba fairly pulsates to the compelling sound of African drums and Spanish guitars. It may be at its most Castilian in Havana and at its most Afro-Caribbean in Santiago de Cuba, but the island rarely rests, and street parties are commonplace. In the 1970s the Uruguayan revolutionary group the Tupamaros adopted the slogan "Everybody dances or nobody dances". In Cuba, at least, this seems to have worked (➤ 6).

Rustic Antiquity

The exquisite, medieval village of **Trinidad** (➤ 106) nestling in the lee of the Escambray Mountains in Central Cuba has been a UNESCO World Heritage Site since 1988. Little has changed in almost five centuries since this, Cuba's third oldest settlement, was founded. A smaller, but no less exquisite gem is the main square of **Remedios** (➤ 116) in Villa Clara Province.

Diving and Snorkelling

Because Castro kept Cuba closed to tourism between 1959 and the early 1990s, Cuba's many dive sites, now open for the first time in decades, are particularly unspoiled. Amongst the best are the Bahía de Corrientes off Guanahacabibes, Cayo Largo in the **Archipiélago de los Canarreos** (➤ 82) and the **Bahía de Cochinos** (➤ 90) west of Cienfuegos.

Unspoiled Scenery

Cuba is full of wonderful drives, walks and treks across as yet undeveloped (and often sparsely settled) territory where the visitor is more likely to see an ox-drawn cart or a cattle train than a tour bus. Of these the long drive through and around the **Sierra Maestra** (➤ 166), taking in **Pico Turquino** (➤ 167), the country's highest peak, and following the unspoiled Caribbean coast eastwards to the ancient city of **Santiago de Cuba** (➤ 134) must rank near the top.

Country farm in the Sierra del Escambray

POSTCARDS
FROM
CUBA

Old World New World
Sugar cane, widely associated with the Caribbean, is in fact not a New World crop but originated in Indonesia. It was first brought to Europe by Arab navigators more than a thousand years ago, and then taken to the Americas by the Spanish in the 16th century. Conversely chilli peppers – so widely associated with Asian cuisine – originated in the Americas and made the same journey but in the opposite direction!

Mermaids
The huge but gentle Caribbean sea cow or manatee (*trichechus manatus*) lives in Cuba's shallow coastal waters and grazes on sea grass. In times past sailors are thought to have mistaken the head and shoulders of manatees rising above the waves for "women of the sea", perhaps giving birth to the legend of mermaids.

Granma
Cuba's population is highly literate, but because of inefficient socialist economics and the US embargo, paper is in such short supply that there is only one regular national newspaper – sometimes – available. This is *Granma*, named after the yacht that brought Castro and his revolutionaries to Cuba in 1956. *Granma Internacional* is published weekly in Spanish, English, French, German and Portuguese.

I Can See For Miles...
On a clear day, from the heights of the Cordillera de la Gran Piedra (▶ 143) near Santiago de Cuba, it's possible to see the neighbouring island of Jamaica. Similarly, on a clear night it's possible to see the lights of nearby Haiti from the lighthouse at Punta de Maisí, Cuba's easternmost headland.

Finding Your Feet

First Two Hours

Arriving By Air

Havana's José Martí International Airport is the main gateway to Cuba. Located **15km (9.3 miles) south of Central Havana**, it has three terminals – Terminal 1 for domestic flights, Terminal 2 for flights bringing Cuban expatriates on holiday from Miami, and Terminal 3 for all other international flights. Most independent travellers will arrive here – there are no international ferry links – but package tourists on "all inclusive" trips may often fly to regional airports such as Camagüey, Cienfuegos, Santiago de Cuba and especially Varadero. In the latter case, all local travel arrangements will have been made in advance by the responsible travel agency.

Customs

■ Independent travellers arriving at José Martí will be pleasantly surprised by the efficiency and modern ambience of the airport. Customs seem strict – there's a personal check, apparently modelled on the former East German system, where the visitor is "closeted" in a small cubicle while credentials are checked. In fact this sounds worse than it is – the **Cuban customs officials tend to be friendly and welcoming**, bearing in mind, no doubt, Fidel Castro's maxim that "tourism is gold". Besides, Cubans tend to be particularly amiable – even the Orwellian-designated "Minint" (Ministry of the Interior) police, much feared by ordinary Cubans, are generally charming to visitors.

■ Items which **cannot legally** be brought into Cuba include narcotics, guns, explosives, pornography, anti-government literature, unprocessed foods and (strangely) pre-recorded video cassettes.

Currency Exchange

■ There's really no need to concern yourself with acquiring Cuban pesos on arrival. **The US$ dollar has already become the universally accepted form of payment** for international visitors, and neither taxi drivers nor hotels will accept anything else – certainly not pesos, unless of the directly convertible variety (➤ 171). Credit cards will do nicely, however – provided the international computer checking system is up and running, which it often isn't!

Tourist Information

■ Unfortunately Cuba isn't big on tourist information. Year-by-year things are gradually changing and improving, but **few cities have official tourist information offices**, and at José Martí International Airport the main purpose of information desks appears to be either selling hotel rooms or providing slightly over-priced limousines for the journey into town.

■ **Getting into Havana** Central Havana is around a 40-minute drive from José Martí International Airport. **Unless you are extremely patient and on a very tight budget, forget all about buses.** Since the collapse of the Soviet Union in 1990 fuel has become extremely scarce in Cuba, and the whole country – even police and military – tend to get about by hitch-hiking. The only real option is to take a taxi – in town these are efficient and metered, but from the airport it's best to fix a price first. US$15 to US$20 is about right for anywhere in downtown Havana.

Car Rental

■ Several **government-owned car rental companies** operate desks at José Martí International Airport. Unless you are very confident it's probably best to forego this option for a day or two until you are familiar both with Cuban driving habits (which are not bad at all) and, more importantly, the layout of the sprawling, underlit and ill-signed city of Havana. Most decent hotels also have car rental desks, and in most circumstances it makes sense to wait a while before renting a vehicle.

■ The most established car rental companies are: **Havanautos** (www.havanautos.cubaweb.cu) and **Transtur** (www.transtur.cubaweb.cu). Rental rates vary, but a good standard figure is around US$50-US$60 per day including insurance (usually unlimited kilometres, but check). If you're seeking to keep the price down, ask about diesel vheicles – the cost of diesel is less than half that of petrol throughout Cuba, and there seem to be more diesel service stations, probably to serve the agriculture industry.

Motorcycle Rental

■ This option is not generally available in Cuba, though **motorbikes and scooters** may be rented at (and within the precincts of) some tourist resort areas, most notably Varadero. Daily rental prices are around half that of car rentals – figure about US$25 a day.

Bicycle Rental

■ **Bikes** can be rented at most tourist resorts for around US$10 a day. There are no official bicycle rental facilities outside resort areas, though it may be possible to rent one privately (and discreetly) from a Cuban family. Check the condition of rental bicycles carefully as most are very run down and facilities for repairs are limited.

Orientation

■ Havana is a surprisingly large city with almost no road signs. Fortunately most taxi drivers are both helpful and at least competent in English – though a little Spanish goes a long way and works wonders in establishing friendly relations. **It's undoubtedly best to have chosen a hotel (perhaps with a fall-back or two) and then simply to ask the driver to take you there.** Beware anyone who tells you the hotel of your choice is "full", "closed" or "no good" – they are simply seeking commissions from their established clients.

On Arrival

■ It's usual for **flights from Europe** (as well as for many from Canada) to arrive in the evening, often around dusk. Under these circumstances it's best to head straight to your hotel and settle in, perhaps venturing out later for a short initial exploration of the Cuban capital. There's a good reason for this – not that Cuba is particularly lawless, rather the contrary – but it *is* dark. There are few street lights, and not all of these work.

Annoyances

■ There are **hustlers** (jineteros) and sometimes prostitutes (jineteras) on just about every side street. Of these the former are by far the worst, offering you everything from illegal cigars to lobsters (an unlikely state monopoly), usually preceded by the assurance: "Friend, I don't want anything". This is a great pity, as most Cubans are honest, educated and anxious to discuss anything from literature to the global economy. But be warned – on the first night, at least, this can be a bit intimidating.

Getting Around

Getting around Cuba isn't hard, but it can be disconcerting and also (especially at night) very dangerous. Not that there's a crime problem – the chances of physical attack are virtually nil, but hitting an unlit tractor or horse-drawn carriage is a very distinct possibility.

Orientation

■ **Road signs**, especially around Havana, are virtually non-existent. This really is a *serious* problem which, hopefully, the government will tackle in the not-too-distant future. Irritatingly there are plenty of signs, of course – but they have nothing to do with road directions and a great deal to do with the inevitable victory of socialism!

Driving

■ Undoubtedly **the best way** to see Cuba is by self-drive car. Numerous government-owned car rental companies exist, and hiring a car is surprisingly simple – all you need is a credit card and an international drivers licence. Driving is on the right, seat belts are compulsory and speed limits are applied fairly rigorously, with on-the-spot fines. The system is quite complex, with speed limits set at 40kph (24.8mph) around schools, 50kph (31mph) in towns, 60kph (37.2mph) on dirt roads, 90kph (55.8mph) on paved highways, and 100kph (62mph) on the motorway or *autopista*.

■ On the one hand, **self-drive in Cuba** is a refreshing change from the clogged motorways of Europe and North America. Traffic – motorised traffic – is very light indeed, due to a combination of the US economic embargo and the near unavailability of fuel. Also, Cubans tend to be careful drivers not least because a car is so valuable a commodity and because spare parts are so hard to come by.

■ On the other hand driving in Cuba can be a nightmare, especially after dark. **Unless it is absolutely necessary to do so, driving after nightfall should be avoided at all costs.**

The *Autopista*

■ Cuba has an **extensive road network** amounting to more than 20,000km (12,400 miles) of paved highways – but most are so narrow that even a bicycle can prevent overtaking in the face of oncoming traffic. The main arterial highway is the *Carretera Central*, built in the 1920s and little upgraded since. There are no drains, and torrential rains can quickly turn the highway into a virtual river.

■ In the 1970s, flushed with the success of the Cuban Revolution, the Castro government began a **programme of building** *autopistas*, or motorways, which were intended to stretch from Pinar del Río in the West to Guantánamo City in the East. About half the network had been completed when the Soviet bloc collapsed in 1990, and little or nothing has been done to improve the network since.

■ Driving the Cuban *autopistas* is a pretty unique experience. To begin with, there's **virtually no traffic** – this is because there is little fuel available, and few people other than dollar-rich tourists can afford to fill their tanks. The downside of this is that every entry and exit point, as well as under bridges, is packed with hitch-hikers who will wander into the road and flag you down with complete abandon. They'll also block the road to try and sell you strings of garlic or pieces of cheese – strictly illegal private enterprise in socialist Cuba – or just stroll across the six-lane highway from one field to another.

■ Add to this **hazards** such as horse-drawn buses, ox carts, farmyard equipment, flocks of sheep, goats and cows – all unlit at night – and the dangers of driving can readily be appreciated. Finally – last but not least – railway tracks, often unmarked, cut across every road in Cuba from the smallest country lane to the *Carretera Central*. Many of these are used for harvesting sugar, but even the main passenger tracks can appear, apparently at random.

Bus
■ *Guaguas* or buses serve most cities in Cuba, but are irregular, overcrowded and generally hot. Watch out, in particular, for the giant hump-backed buses known locally as *camellos*, or camels, which can carry as many as three hundred passengers – but then take a taxi! **Long-distance travel by bus between major tourist destinations is generally fast, efficient and comfortable.** As for local buses or *camiones* – really just converted lorries with standing room only – better to forget them.

Train
■ Cuba is the only Caribbean country with a functioning rail network. And is really does function – not fast, not necessarily on time, and not always very comfortably, but it is **relatively cheap and reliable**. The most enjoyable and practical rail journey is between Havana and Santiago de Cuba, taking around 15 hours and costing just over US$70 to dollar-paying international travellers.

Internal Flights
■ Cuba has a **fairly extensive internal air system** linking all major cities with Havana. There are currently three internal airlines but – as so often is socialist Cuba – this does not mean there is a great deal of competition in prices. Services are slowly improving, but internal flights still rely heavily on ageing and frankly outdated Soviet aircraft. Make reservations through your hotel or at a local travel agency.

Boats and Ferries
■ Several large towns including Havana, Cienfuegos and Santiago de Cuba have local ferries which shuttle regularly across their harbours. **Three different types of vessel** carry passengers between Surgidero de Batabanó in southern Havana Province and Nueva Gerona on the Isla de la Juventud. These include Soviet-made hydrofoils and (rather better) Canadian-made passenger catamarans, both of which make the 100km (62 miles) crossing in around 2 hours. The ageing 500 passenger ferry or *barco* makes the same trip in six hours.

Admission Charges
The cost of admission for museums and places of interest mentioned in the text is indicated by the following price categories:
Inexpensive under US$2   **Moderate** US$2–5   **Expensive** over US$5

Accommodation

Accommodation in Cuba is slowly improving, but still has a long way to go. What's more, it's not likely to improve dramatically under the present system, whereby the government maintains an almost complete monopoly on US$ dollar hotels and does everything in its (very considerable) power to restrict or close down all competition.

Pre-booked Accommodation

■ There's a **theoretical requirement** that all arriving independent tourists should have three nights accommodation pre-booked at a government-approved hotel. You will be asked to fill in your first intended place to stay on the tourist card issued instead of a visa stamp by Cuban embassies the world over, and immigration officials at your airport of arrival may also ask to see your pre-booked hotel voucher. On the other hand, this requirement may very well be ignored. If you're not pre-booking, it's best to be prepared by entering the name of a major government-recognised hotel on your tourist card as a precaution.

Tourist Hotels

■ The Cuban government either owns all tourist hotels in the country or – in **special tourist havens** like Varadero and Cayo Coco – operates a system of licensing under which hotels may be managed by international companies with a high percentage of the profit going to the Cuban state. Generally speaking, ordinary Cubans are not permitted to stay in tourist hotels (few could afford it, in any case), while conversely ordinary tourists are not intended to stay in the inexpensive peso hotels available to Cubans. One important exception to these rules is the Islazul State Agency, a hotel chain that permits both Cubans and foreigners to stay, and which is widely represented across the country.

All-Inclusive Resorts

■ The all-inclusive system is simple – you pay a **fixed price** to your local travel agent for a return flight and a week or two in a resort. This includes a room (usually very comfortable, with facilities such as cable TV), all the food and drink you want in the buffet, restaurants and bars, plus a variety of beach and water activities and evening entertainment. Most resorts cover a large area of landscaped grounds bars, restaurants, swimming pools, gymnasiums, tennis courts and other sports facilities. Generally speaking, the only Cubans permitted on site are those who work there. Very often walk-in tourists are not welcome, either. The system is pretty strictly book in advance.

■ The **major concentrations of all-inclusives** are in Varadero, Cayo Coco and Guardalavaca on the northern (Atlantic) coast, and at Cayo Largo, Playa Ancón, the Jardines de la Reina and Marea del Portillo on the southern (Caribbean) coast. The most positive aspect of the all-inclusive system is that it permits visitors to relax completely within a private enclave. The major drawback is that guests see little and learn less about Cuba outside this enclave. With the exception of Varadero, which is within easy striking distance of Matanzas and Cárdenas, most all-in resorts are geographically remote from Cuban population centres, so that even those who would like to strike out and "see the real Cuba" will find it both difficult and expensive to do so.

Accommodation Agencies

- The Cuban authorities have organised a number of hotel agencies which administer accommodation nation-wide. They look and sound independent and in competition, but they are not. The largest and best organised of these is Horizontes, which operates its own website (www.horizontes.cu) providing detailed information on all its hotels and permitting pre-booking by email. **A print-out of any confirmation of booking** from Horizontes should guarantee the independent traveller entry at José Martí International Airport in case immigration should ask.

Relative Costs

- Besides **Horizontes**, other major government accommodation agencies include **Cubanacán**, **Gaviota**, **Gran Caribe** and **Islazul**. As a general rule, Gaviota tends to be more upmarket, while Islazul is often the most reasonably priced. Still, when additional costs such as breakfast, buffet dinners, parking, etc., are added in, it's surprising how similar prices tend to be across the board.

Joint Enterprises

- Since 1990 all the Cuban government hotel chains have begun to sign joint management agreements with overseas hotel companies such as **Accor** (France), **Iberostar** (Spain), **Qualton** (Mexico), **Sol Melia** (Spain) and **Tryp** (Spain). As a consequence, many seriously run-down hotels have been refurbished, and the standard of accommodation in these joint-venture hotels continues to improve on a yearly basis. The notable absence of US hotel companies from this list means that Cuba's new upmarket hotel scene is decidedly Mediterranean in feel, with Spain definitely leading the way.

Peso Hotels

- There are **cheap hotels and boarding houses** accepting non-convertible pesos all over Cuba, but these are intended for Cubans only and it's very difficult, and getting harder, for non-Cubans to stay in such establishments.

Casas Particulares

- Another theoretical alternative is to stay in private rooms. This became legal back in 1993 when the Cuban authorities started to **permit limited private enterprise**, and rapidly took off as Cubans all over the country converted their homes into little guest houses known as *casas particulares*. Unfortunately it worked too well, and the communist authorities, fearing a major loss of state revenue to the private sector, raised taxes to such an extent that renting private lodgings became economically all but impossible. There are still many *casas particulares*, distinguished by small blue triangles on their front doors, especially in tourist hot spots like Trinidad. As of early 2004, however, the official word was that these would be closing down by government order, so none are recommended in the Where to Stay sections of this book. *Casas particulares* are already completely prohibited in resort areas like Varadero and Cayo Coco.

Prices
The prices below are for a standard double room per night.
$ under US$50 $$ US$50–150 $$$ over US$150

Food and Drink

Cuba doesn't have one of the world's great culinary traditions, but the food is tasty, nutritious and filling. Provision of food isn't a problem – especially for dollar-paying tourists. Cuba has lots of good food – pork, chicken and beef are plentiful, there's fish, crab, prawn and lobster in the warm seas all around the island, and just about any vegetable or fruit will grow with readiness and alacrity in the fertile soil.

Spicing it Up

■ It's hard to understand why Cuban cuisine – *la comida criolla* - should be so bland. It's difficult to avoid crashing into those garlic sellers strolling down the *autopista* – so where is the garlic in the national cuisine? Where are the chilli peppers? If you want to spice things up a bit, **buy a bottle of salsa** and take it to your dining table with you – nobody will object, and it certainly livens things up.

Local Restaurants

■ In fact it's possible for the visitor to eat well in Havana – very well in certain locations – and one can get by comfortably in major cities like Cienfuegos, Camagüey and Santiago de Cuba. It's also possible to eat extremely cheaply – ridiculously cheaply, in fact – by converting some of those tourist dollars into ordinary pesos and joining a queue for **subsidised Cuban food**, though this is almost certainly going to be limited to sausage sandwiches, hamburgers or cheese pizza.

International Restaurants

■ Fortunately, for dollar-wielding visitors, there's no real problem. International standard restaurants are springing up all over the place, but especially in Havana and the major resorts such as Varadero, Cayo Coco, Cayo Largo and Guardalavaca. There are good *criollo* restaurants supplied with **quality provisions** in major cultural centres such as Trinidad, Remedios, Santiago de Cuba and Camagüey, too. Elsewhere it's a different story, and visitors seeking a meal in small provincial towns off the beaten track are likely to find their choice limited to pizza, hamburgers and spaghetti.

Paladares

■ Private restaurants, like private guest houses - *casas particulares* – flourished during the 1990s when Castro allowed limited private enterprise. People were permitted to serve meals in their homes but not to employ staff – it had to be a family-run operation. Unfortunately *paladares*, perhaps the brightest spot in the Cuban culinary scene, were **too successful** and are now being closed down in the same way as the *casas particulares*.

Lots of Meat and some Vegetables

■ Most Cubans like meat – and lots of it. Fried chicken, grilled chicken, pork, beef steak and grilled fish are **enduringly popular**. So to is fresh seafood such as squid, octopus, prawns, crayfish and lobster. The latter, though, can be hard to find – perhaps because the government seeks to maintain a monopoly on the supply of "luxury" seafood, and perhaps because of concerns fishermen may sail away and escape to nearby Florida. The quality of the pork, in particular, is generally excellent. Fresh vegetables are another matter. Salad is indeed available on most menus, but it's as likely to consist of sliced cucumber or cold green beans. Cuban cuisine tends to be as macho as its culture – most people are voracious meat-eaters. Yet nearly every town and city in the country has at least one vegetarian restaurant, and the numbers seem to be increasing.

The Staple Foods

■ To **accompany these delights** are usually fried potatoes, yucca cooked with garlic, or – most promising of all - rice and beans. The latter comes in two varieties, *Moros y Christianos* in the west and centre of the country – "Muslims and Christians" or black beans and white rice, a tradition which must go back a thousand years to the days of Muslim Andalusia - or *congri* in the east of the country, a succulent mix of white rice and red kidney beans.

La Cocina Baracoa

■ Cuba is unusual in not having – with **one notable exception** – any distinctive regional cuisines. Only Baracoa (► 138), in the far east of the country, claims this distinction. There, for example, rice is cooked in coconut milk and more spices are used than in the rest of the country – including annato seeds to colour rice yellow, as well as *tamales* made of mashed plantains and minced pork rather than the usual boiled corn and minced pork.

International Cuisine

■ Dining in Cuba **can be very good** – especially for those on "all inclusive" breaks to resorts like Varadero, Cayo Coco and Playa Ancona. It has been estimated that, for every US$ dollar made from tourism by the Cuban regime, 40 US cents are ploughed back into the trade – and much of this investment is for food. If you're visiting Cuba not as an independent traveller, but strictly as a vacationer, it's not just best, but essential, to book into a hotel that provides three meals a day as well as bed and other services. Here the visitor will find international fare, usually in the form of buffets, which closely parallel those of the Costa Brava in Spain or the Algarve in Portugal.

What to Drink

■ Drinking in Cuba is not a problem. It's best to **avoid tap water** and buy the readily-available bottled varieties – whether still or gaseous. Beer is good and on sale everywhere, though usually in bottles or cans rather than on tap. There's a wide choice of soft drinks, and as for rum (► 9) it's ubiquitous. Wine is available in increasing variety and quality at most of the better restaurants in Havana and other big cities.

Menus, Tipping and Dress Codes

■ Most restaurants in tourist areas have menus in both Spanish and English. Tipping (10 per cent) is increasingly expected and certainly appreciated. Dress codes are **decidedly relaxed**, but most large all-in resorts and luxury hotels will not permit guests to enter the buffet in their swimwear.

Restaurant Prices

Prices in this book are based on the amount you should expect to pay per person for a two-course meal, excluding drinks and service charges.
$ under US$10   **$$** US$10–25   **$$$** over US$25

Shopping

Cuba isn't really a shopper's paradise. A combination of the US embargo and Castro's strict but increasingly illogical socialist economics mean that the island is poorly supplied with goods from overseas, while the development of local handicrafts and arts was long discouraged as symptomatic of private enterprise – an attitude which has only recently begun to change. Nevertheless, there are things to buy in Cuba, and Havana is certainly the best place in the country to go shopping.

Souvenirs
Dollar shops at large hotels sell a variety of souvenirs, none particularly inspiring or inspired, to remind the visitor of Cuba on his or her return home. Enduringly popular – almost sanctified – the image of Ernesto "Che" Guevara decorates everything from T shirts to plates, wooden plaques and a wealth of books by or about the eponymous revolutionary hero. It's also possible to buy Che Guevara posters, postcards and characteristic black berets with the red star of communism on the front. Other souvenirs range from dolls to maracas, coconuts carved into masks or monkeys, leatherwork, woodcarvings and other assorted knick-knacks.

Local Produce
A better bet in the souvenir stakes, also widely available at dollar shops and in large hotels throughout the island, is local produce such as Cuban coffee, cigars and of course rum.

Music
Cuban music (➤ 6) is really one of the island's marvels. In a country that seemingly never stops dancing, a wide range of CDs is available for sale and at very reasonable prices. Music CDs are for sale in shops, on street corners, and musicians performing in bars and hotels will often approach you with recordings of their own work. Definitely a high point in the Cuban shopping scene!

Art
Perhaps because it's clearly a cultural activity, the state doesn't interfere too much in the painting scene. All over the island, but especially in La Habana Vieja and at major tourist attractions, paintings of all kinds – but especially modern art Cuban-style – are for sale at free markets. There are some real bargains to be had, but be prepared to haggle.

Imported Goods
It's really hard to find many everyday things like film, batteries, medicines, even toothpaste and shampoo – except at special government stores in resort areas like Varadero. It's best to bring your own supplies with you. Even simple things like paper and pens can be hard to buy and may entail queuing for quite long periods.

Preserving Nature
Despite its revolutionary nature, the Cuban government doesn't yet seem to have grasped the need to protect the island's natural environment. This means that souvenirs are available made from wild plants, animal parts, stuffed birds, sea shells, coral and even turtle shell. All-in-all, it's best to stay well away from souvenirs of this kind.

Entertainment

Cubans are a fun-loving people, and enjoy any opportunity to relax and forget the economic hardships of the time. Festivals are enduringly popular – especially the Santiago de Cuba carnival. There are frequent concerts of live music, and virtually every town in the country has a *casa de trova* music centre. Whenever they get the chance, Cubans watch the latest films from the United States and Latin America. TV soaps, especially from Brazil and Mexico, are almost a national obsession. Sports feature in a big way in Cuba (► 26), with lots of beach activities like windsurfing and snorkelling. Baseball is by far the most popular sport, though Cubans excel at boxing.

Entertainment for Visitors

Cuba has a wide choice of entertainment options, though few – apart from those designed specifically for well-heeled visitors like the Tropicana Night Club – can be described as particularly up-market. Rather one of the joys of Cuba is the way in which people make their own fun, and welcome visitor participation with real enthusiasm. Options include folk music, jazz clubs, dancing, cabaret shows, discos, theatre, ballet, movies and classical music recitals.

Live Music and Nightclubs

- Ask for the local *casa de trova* in almost any Cuban town and you will be directed to a sort of musical club where Cubans get together to play music and sing, especially at weekends.
- There are **upscale nightclubs** in many all-inclusive resorts and at most large hotels. More down-market, Cubans have their own night scene with disco-dancing and low-priced nightclubs. The latter can sometimes be a bit rough, but visitors are invariably made most welcome.
- In a direct continuation from the pre-revolutionary 40s and 50s, Cuba has a tradition of **gala-style nightclubs** with big bands, leggy showgirls, elaborate costumes and astonishing head-dresses. Havana, Santiago de Cuba and Varadero are the main venues for this kind of entertainment which contrasts strangely with socialist ideology and economic austerity elsewhere in the country.

Cinemas, Classical Concerts and Events Information

- Cuban **cinemas** are pretty run-down and behind-the-times in the range of movies they show. On the other hand they are cheap and friendly.
- Classical music is performed at the *Casa de la Cultura* to be found in every major Cuban town – rather like *salsa* and *sol* may be found at the local *Casa de la Trova*. Cuba prides itself on being a cultured country, and the communist authorities have long sought to promote classical music and ballet.
- For information about **upcoming events** you must rely on the grapevine. There's no monthly or weekly events magazine, no equivalent of *Time Out* or *City Life*, and advertising hoardings are, by and large, limited to revolutionary themes.

Theatres and Circuses

- All of Cuba's provincial capitals boast **theatres** where plays (generally in Spanish) are presented on a regular basis. Children's theatre – a kind of Caribbean pantomime – is enduringly popular, as are puppet shows. Travelling **fun-fares and circuses** are popular with the locals, but your individual safety concerns should be heeded as it will be apparent that the age of the machines and standard of maintenance of fun-fare rides leaves much to be desired.

Entertainment at All-inclusive Resorts

- The all-inclusive resorts make a big effort to make sure their guests have plenty of **activities to choose from**, both in the day and at night. Daytime activities include aerobics in and around the pool, dance lessons, beach volleyball and football, windsurfing, scuba-diving – even (at Varadero) sky-diving. At night there are regular shows featuring singing and dancing, with audience participation actively encouraged.

Sports

- **Baseball** is Cuba's most popular sport, and if you have the opportunity it's well worth going along to a game. Cubans, including Fidel Castro himself, are passionate about baseball.
- The many unspoiled beaches that surround Cuba offer plenty of opportunities for **watersports**. Learn the art of scuba-diving or windsurfing; go snorkelling or diving around coral reefs; join a deep-sea fishing trip or enjoy sailing, surfing or just plain swimming in the warm waters of the Caribbean.
- **Adventure Sports** are not yet a big draw in Cuba, but the future for trekking, climbing, biking and deep sea fishing look bright – it's just a question of time. For the present the Cuban authorities (not exactly well known for their perception of political correctness in the outside world) continue to promote "big game" hunting.

Bars

- There are plenty of bars and drinking spots all over Cuba, most aimed primarily at the local clientele. More **up-market bars** are common in tourist hot-spots like Havana and Varadero, in which case there's nothing to worry about – the authorities make sure that all is above board and undesirable characters are kept out. It's more fun to go local, though, and provided you take sensible precautions against pickpockets there should be no trouble at all. It's a good way to meet the locals, and you may even have trouble paying for that shot of rum – Cubans are a generous bunch, and usually only too happy to make your acquaintance.

Festivals

- Religion is making a comeback in post-Soviet Cuba, and both the major Christian festivals and local Santería festivals are celebrated with increasing openness. Cuba's most famous festival is the Santiago de Cuba **Carnival**, held in the eastern capital between July 25–27 every year, though the celebrations may spill over on either side. This is a celebration in which both locals and, increasingly, visitors let their hair down and enjoy themselves. With samba schools, flower-bedecked floats, scantily- but elaborately-clad dancers, every conceivable kind of Cuban music, rum and beer flowing in quantities – it's the nearest Cuba comes to Brazil. Similar but less authentic celebrations of Carnival are held at Varadero in January and February, and in Havana in November. In both Santiago and Havana locals rehearse every week at *comparsas* or carnival dance schools, and if the visitor is not fortunate enough to be in Santiago de Cuba for the real thing, some idea of what Carnival is like can be gleaned from a visit to one of these.

Havana

Getting Your Bearings

Most visitors to Cuba will arrive in Havana, the country's vibrant but somewhat decaying capital. Cuba's only real metropolis, it's the most important Spanish colonial centre in the whole of Latin America, and a city which fairly shakes and sizzles with excitement. Although both Vedado in the West, and Centro have their share of modern high rise buildings, it's La Habana Vieja – Old Havana, in the east – which is the heart of the city and one of the true glories of Latin America.

Havana is two cities. By day huge, camel-shaped buses carrying as many as 300 passengers vie for space on the pot-holed streets with 50-year-old American jalopies. There's music in the air, and an astonishing range of architectural styles from colonial Spanish to early 20th-century American to delight the eye. To the north, the waves of the Straits of Florida lap or lash against the sea walls, depending on the weather. Everywhere there are national monuments, as well as some of the best museums in North America.

By night Havana is another world, dimly-lit and slightly unnerving, not that there is much real reason for the latter. There's a policeman on virtually every corner, and once you get used to the regular illegal cigar-hustlers and occasional prostitutes – most of whom will respond to a simple *"no me molestes!"* by apologising and disappearing – there really is little to worry about.

Above: *Camello* bus on a Havana street
Left: Old police station sign
Previous page: El Morro seen from the Malecón

Take in Havana's architectural treasures, ancient fortresses, driving musical rhythms and apparently unrestrained love of life. Relax by the sea wall of the Malecón, sip an iced beer or a daiquiri in the ancient Plaza de Armas, or visit the incredible La Tropicana nightclub for a taste of 1950s decadence.

Havana in Three Days

Day One

Morning
Take a taxi to **3 La Habana Vieja** (➤ 54) and just walk the streets of the old town, visiting at least two of the main squares – Plaza de Armas and **11 Plaza de la Catedral** (right, ➤ 62). Lunch at a bistro on **10 Calle Obispo** (➤ 61), or take in the stunning views from Restaurante Mirador de la Bahía above Plaza de Armas.

Afternoon
Continue your exploration of La Habana Vieja, making sure to visit Plaza de San Francisco and Plaza Vieja. Stop for a sundowner at Taberna de la Muralla (➤ 68) on Plaza Vieja and stroll back along Calle Lamparilla (of Graham Greene's *Our Man in Havana* fame).

Evening
Have an early dinner at the excellent Castillo de Farnes (➤ 66) on Calle Monserrate then head out to the **1 Malecón** (➤ 50) for an evening stroll from Castillo de San Salvador de la Punta to Torreón de San Lázaro.

Day Two

Morning
Take a taxi to visit Havana's two great citadels, **4 El Morro** and La Cabaña (➤ 57). Take another taxi back to the **2 Museo de la Revolución** (➤ 52) where you can spend an hour checking out Cuba's recent history. Stroll south down shady **9 El Prado** (➤ 61) for lunch in the neo-Moorish restaurant of the Hotel Inglaterra (➤ 64).

Afternoon
Stroll around **8 Parque Central** (➤ 60) and on to **7 Barrio Chino** (➤ 60), then take a taxi to visit the **6 Cementerio de Colón** (left, ➤ 59).

Evening
Head out, again by taxi, to the up-market western district of Miramar and enjoy drinks, dinner and the fantastic floorshow at Cabaret Tropicana (➤ 72) nightclub.

Day Three

Morning
Hire a car for the day and drive through Havana's eastern outskirts to the small fishing village of **14 Cojímar** (➤ 63) for a seafood lunch at Hemingway's old hangout, the Restaurante La Terrazza de Cojímar (➤ 68).

Afternoon
Drive southwest to the **13 Museo Hemingway** (➤ 63) in the sleepy suburban village of San Francisco de Paula, then continue west to explore the Socialist statuary and open parklands of **12 Parque Lenin** (➤ 62).

Evening
Drive northwest to the upmarket Havana suburb of Vedado, stopping to visit Castro's unexpected tribute to The Beatles, **9 Parque John Lennon** (➤ 59). Next continue to the nearby Playa District and dine at El Aljibe (➤ 66), one of Havana's top *criollo* restaurants.

ⓘ The Malecón

Havana's most famous thoroughfare is the celebrated Malecón, also known as Avenida Antonio Maceo, which runs the length of the capital's considerable seafront with the *Estrecho de la Florida* (Straits of Florida). In many ways the Malecón is Havana – at some time of the day or night all life is here, and just about everyone comes to stroll, sit on the sea wall, fish, swim, gossip or romance.

The Malecón in its present form was constructed under the American administration in 1901. An old Spanish fortification, **Castillo de San Salvador de la Punta** in La Habana Vieja, marks the eastern end. From here it runs westwards for 8km (5 miles) through Central Havana to **Castillo de la Chorrera**, another small Spanish fortress marking the boundary between Vedado and Miramar districts.

The eastern end of the Malecón has fine views of the great fortress of El Morro (▶ 57) which guards the entrance to Havana Harbour. In this area, during the colonial era, large tanks for bathing or washing were cut into the solid rock just offshore. Walking west the once grand houses of Central Havana line the route as far as the Monumento Antonio Maceo, dedicated to the memory of the great independence fighter. Close by the Torreón de San Lázaro was once a Spanish watchtower.

Monument to the Maine

About 1.5km (0.9 mile) further west the Hotel Nacional dominates the skyline. Nearby is the **Monumento al Maine**, originally built to honour the victims of the mysterious but convenient explosion which sank the *USS Maine* in 1898 and provided an excuse for the Spanish-American War later in the same year. The monument, complete with cannons from the Maine recovered from the bay, was once topped by an American eagle, but today bears the inscription (in Spanish, on the marble tablet in front) "To the victims of the *Maine* who were sacrificed by voracious imperialism in its desire to seize Cuba".

The Monument to the *Maine*

Ten minutes' walk west of the Maine Monument, and the last major attraction on the Malecón before La Chorrera, is the impressive **Monumento Calixto Garcia**, dedicated to another great revolutionary hero. The monument features 24 bronze plaques detailing Garcia's 30-year struggle in the late 19th century against the Spanish. There are fine views across the Bay and east towards El Morro.

TAKING A BREAK

For a prime view both ways along the Malecón try the **Hotel Nacional** (► 65). This landmark serves pretty good food and also permits non-guests dining here to use the hotel's large outdoor pool.

The Malecón looking westwards to the Hotel Nacional

🔛 178 C4

✉ Avenida Antonio de Maceo

THE MALECÓN: INSIDE INFO

Top tips If exploring the Malecón on foot it makes sense to **stick to the northern sidewalk**, next to the sea, for most of the way. Driving is another matter; from east to west you see the waterfront, but from west to east, you'll be further inland, and will see much less of the shore. It's probably best to drive the Malecón both ways, starting and finishing at the eastern end.

• **Watch out for hustlers** at all times, prostitutes who can be pushy at night, and – more dangerous and harder to avoid than either of the former – deep pot-holes at places in the badly eroded sidewalk.

• During bad weather and the hurricane season in September **huge waves** can batter the sea wall, drenching the Malecón and anybody walking along it.

2 Museo de la Revolución

Fittingly the Museum of the Revolution is housed in the former palace of Cuban dictator Fulgencio Batista, overthrown by Fidel Castro in 1959. The building was constructed between 1913 and 1920 in grand neo-classical style, and the interior was decorated by Tiffany's of New York. It is a beautiful building, and is worth a visit for the architecture as much as for the revolutionary artefacts gathered both within and round about.

Part of the museum is devoted to the revolutionary exploits of Cuban nationalists during the Wars of Independence, and the grand stairway is dominated by a bust of José Martí, the father of the nation, as well as by a Cuban

flag. The exhibits are laid out on three floors connected by a monumental marble stairway rising to an **impressive dome** patterned with fine ceramic tiles. Immediately beneath this is a heroic but less artistically accomplished mural of Cuban independence fighters battling the Spanish in the Wars of Independence. Another impressive architectural feature is the **Salón de los Espejos** (Room of Mirrors), a great reception room on the first floor leading to three balconies from which

The Museo de la Revolución was once the Cuban presidential palace

Batista – and Cuban presidents and dictators before him – used to address the people.

Also of historical merit and unrelated to the revolutionary events is the **Baluarte del Ángel**, a surviving watchtower from the old city wall, now somewhat overshadowed by the SAU-100 Soviet tank parked next to it. This vehicle is supposedly the tank used by Fidel Castro in his successful defeat of the Bay of Pigs invasion in 1961. Most of the exhibits within the museum relate directly to the Cuban Revolution of 1959 and especially to the heroic endeavours of Camilo Cienfuegos, Ernesto "Che" Guevara and Fidel Castro. Elsewhere in the country there isn't a very visible Fidel personality cult, but here, at the museum, Fidel certainly features.

Revolutionary History

The exhibits give a detailed record of the events leading to the overthrow of Batista, from the initial attack on the Moncada Barracks in 1953 (➤ 20) through to recent times. Visitors should be aware that there is an almost sanctified feel to the salons exhibiting the guns, bombs, bloodstained uniforms, detailed military maps and pictures of martyrs; curators tend to follow visitors about in case they show insufficient respect or even touch something.

Outside is the equally hallowed **Granma Memorial**. Here there is a replica of the yacht *Granma*, used by Fidel and his revolutionaries to land in Oriente in 1956. It's housed in a particularly ugly building, and condensation makes it difficult to see through the surrounding glass walls. Scattered around are various other vehicles used in the revolution including a bus that carried munitions and a bulldozer converted to become a tank. It's under permanent military guard, and once again the atmosphere is reverential.

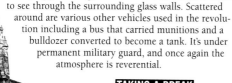

TAKING A BREAK

Head east into La Habana Vieja and look for Hemingway's old hangout, **La Bodeguita del Medio** (➤ 67), just a short stroll away on Calle Empedrado.

🚩 179 E4
✉ Calle Refugio 1, between Agramonte and Avenida de las Misiones ☎ (7) 862-4091
🕐 Tue–Sun 10–5 💰 Moderate

MUSEO DE LA REVOLUCIÓN: INSIDE INFO

Don't miss El Rincón de los Cretinos (Cretin's Corner) on the way out of the museum near the gift shop features life-sized caricatures of politicians particularly despised or hated by the Cuban revolution.

3 La Habana Vieja

La Habana Vieja (Old Havana) is the most important and exciting attraction in all Cuba. It was declared a National Monument in 1977, and a UNESCO World Heritage Site in 1982, but restoration of this, the most significant centre of Spain's colonial heritage in all the Americas, has been painfully slow. At present the heart of La Habana Vieja, which lies in the northern part of the Old City, is already sufficiently restored to be truly marvellous. The south, a possibly dangerous slum area, and should be avoided.

Old Havana is dominated by four main squares linked by a narrow grid of colourful cross-streets which are gradually being cobbled and restored. They are all within easy walking distance, and it's best to start in the **Plaza de Armas**, which dates from 1582 and is the oldest square in the city. Approached from Central Havana by **Calle Obispo** (➤ 61), this shady square has been almost completely restored and is home to a number of fine colonial buildings, good restaurants and a lively second-hand book market.

Immediately to the northeast side of the square is the **Castillo de la Real Fuerza**, the oldest colonial fortress in the New World. The weathervane on top of the west tower is a female figure, **La Giraldilla**, which has become the symbol of Havana. This is a replica - the original, dating from 1632, is in the baroque **Museo de la Ciudad** on the west side of Plaza de Armas. In the centre of the square is a statue of Cuban national hero **Carlos Manuel de Céspedes** (➤ 14). Often there is live music in the square, with Santería (➤ 16) women from Oriente dancing

Flower girl and old colonial bell in the Plaza des Armas

to Afro-Cuban rhythms – expect to pay US$1 if you want to take pictures. The rooftop **Restaurante Mirador de la Bahía** offers live music, good pizzas and, as its name suggests, an unparalleled view of the Bahía de la Habana and Havana Harbour.

Colonnaded building on the east side of the Plaza Vieja

Other Squares

About 200m (218 yards) to the south is the **Plaza de San Francisco**, with some of the most attractive colonial houses in Old Havana and, most notably, the **Iglesia y Convento de San Francisco de Asís**, no longer a church but a concert hall and museum of religious art. The church tower at 36m (118ft) is the tallest in Havana, and there's an attractive modern bronze statue of St Francis on the pavement outside. A white marble fountain, the **Fuente de los Leones** (Fountain of Lions) dominates the centre of the square.

On the south side of the Iglesia San Francisco is **Parque Humboldt**, named after the German explorer Alexander Von Humboldt. His house, the **Casa Alejandro von Humboldt**, exhibits displays of his contribution to the cataloguing of Cuba's fauna and flora in the 19th century. The nearby **Museo del Ron** (Museum of Rum) is also worth a visit.

Just 100m (109 yards) west of the Plaza de San Francisco is the third of Old Havana's distinguished squares, **Plaza Vieja**, dating from the mid-16th century – it was once the capital's main slave market. This magnificent square is currently under restoration, with the northern and eastern sides of the plaza restored to their former glory. There's a good restaurant with sheltered outdoor seating at **El Portal del San Angelo**, housed in the former **Colegio San Angelo** – a fine colonnaded colonial structure dating from 1866. On the south of the square the **Casa de los Condes de Jaruco** has a broad covered gallery dating from the 1730s which is being developed as a cultural shopping mall with art galleries and craft shops.

Narrow Back Streets

Apart from the four main squares – which include the spectacular **Plaza de la Catedral** (► 62) – virtually every narrow street in Old Havana is resplendent with architectural gems reflecting Cuba's Hispanic colonial past. Two impressive examples are the parallel north-south **Calle Oficios** and **Calle Mercaderes**, running between Obispo and Muralla. It's best just to wander these back streets – which are very safe, with a policeman on almost every corner. The architecture and the sense of history is spectacular, but maybe Old Havana's greatest attraction is the endless variety of street performers and street people, from dreadlocked Rastas and Santería priestesses through nattily dressed dancers to *salsa* and *sol* bands, wandering guitarists and traditionally dressed flower girls.

Iglesia y Convento de San Francisco de Asis

TAKING A BREAK

Try the **Taberna de la Muralla** (► 68) on Plaza Vieja, a tastefully decorated colonial period pub with its own microbrewery

Iglesia y Convento de San Francisco de Asis
- 179 F4
- Calle Oficios
- (7) 862-3467
- Daily 9:30–7
- Moderate

Casa Alejandro von Humboldt
- 179 F3
- Calle Oficios 254
- (7) 863-9850
- Tue–Sun 9:30–6
- Inexpensive

LA HAVANA VIEJA: INSIDE INFO

Top tips Take it easy – Old Havana isn't for rushing. Stop for a cool drink in any or all of the four squares and enjoy the **musical ambience** and the incredible street life.

- **Visit the art market** at the junction of Calle Tacón and Calle Empedrado where there's lots of colourful styles on show.
- **Casa de los Árabes** at Calle Oficios 16 celebrates Arab and Islamic culture in Cuba.

4 El Morro and La Cabaña

Two castles, Castillo de los Tres Santos Reyes del Morro (El Morro) and Fortaleza de San Carlos de la Cabaña (La Cabaña) dominate the narrow entrance to the Bahía de la Habana and Havana Harbour. Together they form the single largest Spanish military complex in the Americas, reinforcing Havana's position as the most important repository of Spain's colonial legacy in the New World.

Battlements at
El Morro

El Morro, at the northern entrance to the bay, was constructed between 1560 and 1630. It's a massive stone fortress on a sheer limestone headland which dominates the view east from The Malecón (► 50) and with its 3m (9.8ft) thick walls must once have seemed all but impregnable. Nevertheless, it was taken by storm by the English in 1762 and held for 11 months. When they eventually withdrew, the Spanish determined to strengthen the defences of the capital by building the even more massive La Cabaña slightly to the south. On being informed of the huge size of this fortress, King Carlos II of Spain is said to have tried to see it through a telescope, commenting jokingly that because of its massive cost it must surely be visible from Madrid!

Today El Morro is visited mainly because of the fantastic views it offers across Havana. There's a lively handicrafts and paintings market at the entrance to the fortress. Guarding the bay below is the impressive **Baluarte de los Doce Apóstoles** (Battery of the Twelve Apostles), named after the 12 cannons mounted there since the days of the Spanish-American War. The former ammunition store is now a small bar, **El Polvorín** (The Powder House).

A Powerful Fortress

La Cabaña is grander and more powerful than El Morro, but it lacks the fantastic view across the Straits of Florida. It does, however, offer stupendous views west across La Habana Vieja and beyond. Built between 1763 and 1774 – it was started just months after the troublesome English departed El Morro – La Cabaña is large, covering 10ha. Its stone ramparts are 12m (40ft) thick in some parts, and the fortress has never been taken in battle. Today it houses a small Cuban military detachment, the **Museo de Fortificacions y Armas**, and has the air of a small village, with cobbled streets and rows of buildings sheltering behind the mighty ramparts.

Like the Castillo de San Pedro del Morro (► 142) in distant Santiago de Cuba, a cannon is fired at La Cabaña every night at 8.45 by soldiers dressed in the traditional uniform worn by Cuban troops fighting the Spanish in the wars of independence. It's wise to get there half an hour early for a good viewpoint.

Cannonballs at Fortaleza de San Carlos de la Cabaña with El Morro in the distance

TAKING A BREAK

There's the small **El Polvorin** bar at El Morro, but much more comfortable is the **Restaurante La Divina Pastora** at La Cabaña, offering fresh seafood from the nearby Straits of Florida.

El Morro	La Cabaña
✚ 179 E5	✚ 179 F5
✉ Calle Oficios	✉ Calle Oficios 254
☎ (7) 862-3467	☎ (7) 863-9850
🕐 Daily 9:30–7	🕐 Tue–Sun 9:30–6
🍴 Moderate	🍴 Inexpensive

EL MORRO & LA CABAÑA: INSIDE INFO

Top tips Most visitors content themselves with a visit to El Morro. This is a mistake as La Cabaña is the more interesting of the two and – especially during the **mornings** – much less crowded with tour buses.

• Climb **El Morro's lighthouse** for the best views of the city.

At Your Leisure

5 Parque John Lennon

Nothing much happens in Cuba without the approval of *El Jefe Maximo*, Fidel Castro. It's fair to assume, then, that Fidel approves of the words and sentiment behind John Lennon's famous song *Imagine*.

John Lennon statue

This is both interesting and indicative of a genuine internationalism. It's difficult to believe either Stalin or Mao Zedong would have approved lyrics urging mankind to "imagine there's no countries... nothing to kill or die for". Yet that's exactly what Parque John Lennon is all about.

In this quiet, shady park, a life-size bronze of the famous Beatle sits casually on a park bench. Inscribed on a plaque in front of him, in Spanish, are the emotive words: *diran que soy un sonada, pero no soy el unier* – "you may say I'm a dreamer, but I'm not the only one". It's moving, optimistic and draws many visitors. Indeed so many that there's now a 24-hour security guard, as John's glasses have been stolen twice!

✚ 178 A3 ✉ Between Calle 15/17 and Calle 6/8, Vedado

6 Cementerio de Colón

Also known as the Necropolis Cristobal Colón, the Spanish name for Christopher Columbus, this is Havana's – and Cuba's – most important cemetery. It's a vast marble city of the dead, though claims that a million people are interred here seem scarcely credible. Entry is through a grand neo-classical gateway.

Established in 1871, the cemetery is laid out in a grid design with a fine octagonal chapel (1886) at the centre. Many of the graves and mausoleums are finely and elaborately executed in marble or granite, and some of Cuba's greatest leaders and richest families lie entombed here. Perhaps most celebrated of all in the tomb of Señora Amelia Goyri, who died in childbirth during 1901. It is believed that she was buried with the child beside her, but when disinterred for reburial the child was miraculously in her arms. Today it's the centre of a popular cult and the tomb is covered with wreaths and flowers.

🕂 178 A2 ⊠ Main entrance on Zapata and Calle 12, Vedado 🕐 Daily 8–4:30 💷 Inexpensive ❓ A guidebook with a detailed map (US$5) is available at the ticket office

7 Barrio Chino

Large numbers of Chinese labourers came to Cuba around 1850; most were from Guangdong Province and came to work in the sugar fields and build railroads. A second wave arrived during the 1870s, fleeing anti-Chinese sentiment and legislation in California. Finally, a third wave took refuge here during the years of turmoil surrounding the overthrow of the Qing Dynasty in 1911. By the beginning of the 20th century the ethnic Chinese population of Cuba had reached around 50,000, and Havana's Chinatown or Barrio Chino was the largest in Latin America.

Very few of these Chinese migrants were women, so over the intervening years intermarriage and, subsequently, emigration to the United States has reduced the number of "Chinese Cubans" to

around 500. Today a movement to rediscover Barrio Chino's Chinese traditions is under way and the area around Calle Cuchillo and San Nicolas is distinguished by a Chinese gateway and a few small Chinese restaurants. There's also a Chinese Cemetery on Calle 26 at the southwestern corner of the Cementerio de Colón.

🕂 179 E3 ⊠ Between Calles Zanja and Rayo, Centro

8 Parque Central

Parque Central divides La Habana Vieja from Centro and is the location both of some very distinguished architecture as well as some of Cuba's finest 1950s-era American Cadillacs. Many of these are parked awaiting customers outside the Hotel Inglaterra, one of Havana's best hotels with a fine, neo-baroque façade (and a rare internet café). Immediately to the south is the splendid Gran Teatro, a fabulously ornate building dating from 1837 with several auditoriums and a dance hall; both the National Ballet of Cuba and the State Opera are based here. In the square opposite, surrounded by fine specimens of royal palms, is a white marble statue of José Martí (► 15).

Immediately south of Parque Central is the vast and grandiose **Capitolio**, built in the 1920s and modelled unashamedly on the Capitol in Washington DC. Immediately behind (to the west) of the Capitolio, don't miss the fine **Fábrica de Tabacos Partagás** building; this famous cigar factory offers two guided tours a day.

🕂 179 E4 ⊠ Capitolio 🕐 Daily 8–8 💷 Moderate

Barrio Chino, Havana's Chinatown

Fábrica de Tabacos Partagás
✉ Calle Industria 520 🕐 Mon–Sat 9–5
💲 Expensive

9 El Prado

North of Parque Central a major
boulevard, Paseo de Martí – better
known as El Prado – runs north to
the Malecón. Dating from the late
18th century, it was once home to
Havana's richest and most powerful
families, and this is reflected in the
ornate architecture. By the beginning
of the 20th century the area was

10 Calle Obispo

This is perhaps the most famous
street in La Habana Vieja. It was the
first to be restored after the Old City
became a UNESCO World Heritage
site, and has now been cobbled and
made into a pedestrian-only zone.
Today it's a great place to sit at one of
the numerous street-side cafés or
bistros and to visit art galleries, and
shops selling imported clothing and
better-quality souvenirs - but only if
you have dollars. This really is "up-
market" Old Havana, and the few

The impressive façade of the Capitolio

already in serious decline, and much
of the Prado had become a red light
area, with scantily dressed girls
standing on the elaborately decorated
first-floor balconies to lure in
customers.

Today the Prado is gradually being
restored. A long, tree-shaded central
walk ornamented with marble lions
and statues of various national
heroes enhances the beauty of the
colonial architecture.

➕ 179 E4 ✉ Between La Punta Fort
and Parque Central

remaining peso shops are rapidly disappearing.

Walking east down Obispo watch
out for the Banco Nacional de Cuba
at the junction with Calle Cuba, the
Hotel Florida with its fine interior
courtyard, and two wonderful old
pharmacies, the Droguería Johnson
on the junction with Aguiar and, a
little further east, the Farmacia y
Droguería Taquechel – note the
skeleton in a glass case visible

Interior of Catedral de la Habana

through the window! At the eastern end of Obispo, at the junction with Mercaderes, is the Hotel Ambos Mundos where Ernest Hemingway lived for some years in the 1930s and wrote *For Whom The Bell Tolls*. For a small fee you can visit his room, No. 511.

➕ 179 F4 ✉ La Habana Vieja

🄻 Plaza de la Catedral

Perhaps the most delightful of Old Havana's squares, this cobbled open area (pedestrians only) is surrounded by fine buildings and home to the most colourful of all La Habana Vieja's street people and performance artists. They range from Santería priestesses through sharp-suited street dancers to flower girls and Rastafarians – all of whom will want around US$1 if you wish to photograph them.

The splendid baroque Catedral de la Habana, dating from 1777, dominates the square. Officially the Catedral de la Virgen María de la Concepción Immaculada, the great, brass-bound wooden doors are

particularly impressive – locals rap them for good luck at New Year! Other fine buildings around the square include the Casa del Marques de Arcos, today an art gallery, and the Casa de Lombillo (1741) which now houses the Museo de la Educación. Directly opposite the cathedral is the fully restored Casa del Conde de Casa Bayona (1720), a fine colonial building which contains the Museo de Arte Colonial.

➕ 179 F4 ✉ La Habana Vieja
🕐 Cathedral: Mon–Sat 10–4, Sun 9–12

🄻 Parque Lenin

This large park and playground about 20km (12.4 miles) south of central Havana is popular with locals at weekends. An area comprising nearly 700ha (1,729 acres) of parkland, lakes and woods, it's home to one of the world's increasingly rare monuments to Soviet revolutionary hero V.I. Lenin. There's also a rather touching bronze memorial to Celia Sanchez, first woman of the Cuban

Revolution and Fidel Castro's close confidante, who died in 1981. Attractions in the immediate vicinity – if you have a taxi or your own transport – include the 600ha (1,482 acres) Járdin Botánico Nacional, the Parque Zoológico Nacional and ExpoCuba, a huge permanent exhibition housed in 25 pavilions displaying Cuba's economic and scientific achievements since the 1959 revolution.

This whole area is Havana's "green lung" and an excellent place to escape from the hurly-burly to city life.

🕂 181 E4 ✉ 20km (12.4 miles) south of central Havana, Arroyo Naranjo
🚊 Galápago de Oro Station
👜 Inexpensive

🔟 Museo Hemingway

In 1939 American writer Ernest Hemingway packed his bags and left Hotel Ambos Mundos (➤ 64) where he had lived for several years. He moved to a large house, Finca Vigía, which he bought in the suburban village of San Francisco de Paula 10km (6.2 miles) south of central Havana. Here he was to live until he finally left Cuba, just a year before his death in 1961. Today the house is preserved as the Museo Hemingway, much as the writer left it, with thousands of books, numerous stuffed animals and the author's typewriter and Mannlicher carbine. Unfortunately visitors are not permitted to enter the building, but may only peer in through open windows and doors.

🕂 181 E4 ✉ 15km (9.3 miles) southeast of central Havana, on Calle Vigía, San Francisco de Paula ⊕ Mon, Wed–Sat 9–4, Sun 9–12:30
👜 Moderate

🔢 Cojímar

This small fishing village is famous for its long association with Ernest Hemingway. It was here that he liked to go deep-sea fishing, and here that he conceived and partially wrote *The Old Man and the Sea* – indeed the supposed model for this role, Hemingway's fishing companion and friend Gregorio Fuentes, still lived at Cojímar until recently.

Today a visit to Cojímar revolves around Hemingway. The Hemingway Memorial featuring the author's bust stands by the seafront, near the old Spanish bastion Torreón de Cojímar (1649), and – perhaps of most interest to the visitor – Hemingway's old bar, the Restaurante La Terrazza, has been converted into a good seafood restaurant, packed with Hemingway memorabilia.

🕂 181 E4 ✉ 10km (6.2 miles) northeast of Havana on the road to the Playas del Este

Hemingway statue at Cojímar

Where to... Stay

Prices
Expect to pay per double room per night
$ under US$50 $$ US$50–150 $$$ over US$150

Ambos Mundos $$

Built in the 1920s, this modest but comfortable hotel is ideally located for Old Havana and is also a part of the Hemingway Trail. The great man lived here for several years during the 1930s and his room – No. 511 – is now preserved as a small museum which you can visit even if you're not staying at the hotel. There's a piano bar offering good live music nightly and a fine antique elevator takes you to a second bar on the roof. Good views across La Habana Vieja to the harbour and El Morro and La Cabaña beyond.

🖪 179 F4 🖂 Calle Obispo 153, La Habana Vieja ☎ (7) 609529; fax: (7) 609532; diana@mundo.cu

Deauville $$

A large, clean and functional hotel well-placed for the Malecon and La Habana Vieja which is popular with mid-budget travellers. Facilities include a swimming pool, a 6th-floor restaurant with good views over the city and criollo food, a disco and a souvenir shop. Recommended for location and price rather than character.

🖪 179 E4 🖂 Avenida de Italia (Galiano) on the Malecón ☎ (7) 338813; fax: (7) 338148

Florida $$$

A wonderful hotel set in a restored 18th-century mansion in the heart of Old Havana. There's a lot of period atmosphere both in the finely furnished rooms and in the colonial-style arches and pillars surrounding the cool central courtyard. Florida's stylish restaurant offers quality criollo and international cuisine, also a piano bar with live music nightly.

🖪 179 F4 🖂 Calles Obispo and Cuba, La Habana Vieja ☎ (7) 8624127; fax: (7) 8624117; commercial@habaguanexhflorida.co.cu

Habana Libre $$

This high-rise hotel in downtown Vedado dates from the 1950s. Apart from its superb location, the Habana Libre is also popular with visitors because of the wide range of services it offers. These include a 2nd-floor swimming pool, the Turquino Cabaret on the 25th floor, a business centre (telephone and email), banking facilities, car rental services, a taxi stand and numerous shops including a photography shop and a book shop.

🖪 178 C4 🖂 Calle L between Calles 23 and 25, Vedado ☎ (7) 334011; fax: (7) 33141; reservath@solmeliacuba.com

Inglaterra $$

Next to the Gran Teatro and overlooking Parque Central, the Ingalterra was erected in 1875 and remains noteworthy for its fine period architecture and elaborate Moorish-style lobby and restaurant. There's a rooftop bar with live music and a useful business centre with (by current Cuban standards) an efficient email and internet service. Banking facilities, car rental services and a nearby taxi stand add to the convenience of staying at this hotel.

🖪 179 E4 🖂 Paseo de Martí (Prado) 416, Parque Central ☎ (7) 608593; fax: (7) 608254; reserva@gcingla.gca.tur.cu

Lido $

Very much at the budget end of Havana accommodation, the Lido is in the run-down Colón District between Ánimas and Trocadero. There's a cafeteria off the lobby and a rooftop restaurant on the 5th floor serving tasty but limited Cuban fare such as pork steak, French fries and grilled chicken. The staff are friendly, the place is clean and it remains one of the cheapest places to stay in Centro de Habana.

➕ 179 E4 ⊠ Calle Consulado 216, between Calles Ánimas and Trocadero, Centro ☎ (7) 338814

Lincoln $-$$

Built in 1926, when it was the second tallest building in Havana, this hotel still has a very period feel to it. The rooms are comfortable and there's a rooftop restaurant for breakfast (with excellent views both across the city and of the nearby Straits of Florida) and a lobby restaurant for buffet meals that opens at lunch and in the evening. There's a nightclub with a floor show on the rooftop every night.

The Lincoln is something of a standby for regular visitors to Havana, journalists and writers. Facilities include currency exchange and car rental services. As with many Cuban hotels, the credit card verifier rarely works at weekends. Well located for the Malecón and La Habana Vieja.

➕ 179 E4 ⊠ Calle Virtudes 164, Avenida de Italia ☎ (7) 338209; fax: (7) 8638743

Nacional $$$

Havana's pre-eminent hotel (at least in size and prestige) since the 1930s, the Nacional dominates the central Malecón and the Vedado skyline from the bay. It's big and among its numerous facilities are two swimming pools, a business centre, tennis courts, barber shop, pharmacy, banking (including advances on MasterCard and Visa), car rental and a guarded parking lot. Rooms are unexceptional, but there are attractive gardens. Famous people who have stayed here

include Winston Churchill, Frank Sinatra and Ava Gardner. The location is central, the views superb and the menu fine but limited. The overall feel is a touch run-down.

➕ 178 C4 ⊠ Calles O and 21, Vedado ☎ (7) 333564; fax (7) 335054, reserva@gnacio.gca.tur.cu

Riviera $$

The Riviera is an old gangster's hotel, built by the "Jewish Godfather" Meyer Lansky (▶ 18) in 1957, just two years before Castro's revolution drove him to retirement in the nearby Bahamas. Some of the rooms have good views of the Straits of Florida. Unusually, there are a few rooms with special facilities for disabled visitors. Facilities include a lobby bar, restaurant, swimming pool, coffee shop by the pool, car rental facilities and money exchange. Because of the location, you'll need to use taxis to visit La Habana Vieja or Vedado. A high point is the music at the Riviera's nightclub, the

Palacio de Salsa. The buffet restaurant, though perfectly adequate, offers a rather limited choice.

➕ 178 A4 ⊠ Avenida Paseo and Malecón, Vedado ☎ (7) 334051; fax: (7) 333739; reserva@gcrivie.gca.tur.cu

Santa Isabel $$$

Probably the best hotel in Havana, if not all Cuba. Originally the Palacio de los Condes de Santovenia, the building – dating from the early 19th century – became a hotel in 1867 which General Domingo Santovenia returned to Spain. It was upgraded to five-star status in 1995, an unusually luxurious standard for Cuba. Today the building exudes elegance, style and comfort. Located on the historic Plaza des Armas, many rooms offer fine views across the heart of La Habana Vieja.

➕ 179 F4 ⊠ Calle Baratillo 9, Plaza de Armas, La Habana Vieja ☎ (7) 608201; fax: (7) 8624127, commercial@habaguanexhisabel.co.cu

Where to...
Eat and Drink

Prices

Expect to pay per person for a two-course meal, excluding drinks and service
$ under US$10 $$ US$10–25 $$$ over US$25

Al Medina $$

Set in a beautifully restored colonial mansion, this is one of Havana's top Middle Eastern restaurants featuring Arab dishes based on lamb and couscous, mezze, hummus, falafel and kebab. The menu is also filled out with criollo specialities, though this is true more-or-less everywhere in Cuba. The Arab cuisine is primarily Lebanese, but the presence of couscous indicates a Maghrebi influence that is a pleasant diversion from the ordinary.

🚹 179 F4 ⊠ Calle Oficios 12, Calles Obispo and Obrapia, La Habana Vieja ☎ (7) 8671041 ⏰ Daily noon–10

Castillo de Farnes $$

An unassuming café on the corner of Monserrate conceals a small but elegant air-conditioned restaurant with friendly, English-speaking staff. Close by Parque Central, this is a little oasis with (by local standards) a fine selection of wines from Spain, France and Argentina as well as Cuba. The ambience is enhanced by an art deco interior as well as by framed black-and-white pictures of Fidel Castro, Raul Castro and Ernesto "Che" Guevara eating and drinking here during the early days of the revolution. The menu features criollo cuisine as well as a selection of hors d'oeuvres including prawn cocktail.
Specialities include Catalan-style chorizo con patatas en salsa (sausage and potatoes in a rich tomato and onion sauce), bacalao a la llauna (salted cod) and especially lobster seethed in its own juices. A good filet de chateaubriand is also served. Male guests receive a cigar gratis with the bill.

🚹 179 E4 ⊠ Calles Monserrate and Obrapia, La Habana Vieja ☎ (7) 8671030 ⏰ Daily noon–midnight

El Aljibe $$

El Aljibe an up-market restaurant catering to the Cuban élite, business people, diplomats and affluent tourists, is enduringly popular and is certainly one of the best state-run restaurants serving Cuban criollo dishes. House specialities include barbecued chicken and beef brocheta, served with unusually tender Moros y Christianos (black beans and rice) and simple but fresh green salad. Although it's a large restaurant, El Aljibe has an intimate atmosphere. Service is friendly and fast, though when the restaurant is full it can be slow.

🚹 181 E4 ⊠ 71 Avenida 7, Calles 24 and 26, Miramar ☎ (7) 2041583/4 ⏰ Daily noon–midnight

El Portal del Sante Ángel $$

Set in an attractive restored colonial building, formerly the Colegio El St Angelo founded in 1866, this restaurant overlooks Old Havana's Plaza Vieja. You can eat inside or on the colonnaded terrace outside. Dishes include pollo a la Cubana (Creole-style chicken), as well as especialidades de la casa tablas (house specialities) such as pescados (fish), mariscos (seafood) and embutidos (sausage) platters. Perhaps most noteworthy is the delicious muelitas de cangrejo con miel y ajo, or crab claws with honey and garlic.

🚹 179 F4 ⊠ Plaza Vieja and Calle San Ignacio, La Habana Vieja ☎ (7) 8611626 ⏰ Daily 8 am–1 am

La Bodeguita del Medio $$

An old Hemingway haunt distinguished by black-and-white pictures of the author. A deliberately Bohemian feel is cultivated with the walls covered with graffiti. The location near Plaza Vieja and the literary associations bring in many sightseers. To escape this more-or-less constant flow, try the quieter and more comfortable roof terrace. Creole cuisine is the house speciality, and it's good. The *ajiaco* (pork and vegetable stew) with rice is to be recommended, but the troubadours who will hang around your table until tipped can be an irritation.

➕ 179 F4 ⊠ Calle Empedrado 207, between Calles San Ignacio and Cuba, La Habana Vieja ☎ (7) 338857 ⊛ Daily 10.30 am–1 am

La Dominica $$

This predominantly Italian restaurant specialises in pasta dishes (usually variants of spaghetti) and pizza, but also offers a varied selection of Cuban *criolla* dishes – the beefsteak is unusually succulent and tender. It is renowned for its lobster, though it's not cheap. The establishment is under foreign management, and this is reflected both in the ambience and the better-than-average service. The location is excellent for strolling in La Habana Vieja, and it's a good place to sit and watch Cuban life go by over an iced beer.

➕ 179 F4 ⊠ Calle O'Reilly 108 and Mercaderes, La Habana Vieja ☎ (7) 602918 ⊛ Daily noon–midnight

La Giraldilla $$$

A reliable, top-end of the market restaurant. There's a Madrid-style *tapas* bar and attractive open-air terrace restaurant called El Patio los Naranjos (The Patio of Oranges). The wine list in the excellent basement Spanish restaurant called La Bodega del Vino is extensive, and includes European and New World vintages as well as local Cuban produce. It's attractively decorated with a timbered ceiling and antique-style ornaments and furniture and there's a live cabaret most evenings. Try the prawns steeped in garlic and flame-grilled lobster served with a Ricard sauce.

➕ 181 E4 ⊠ Calles 222 and 37, La Lisa ☎ (7) 330568 ⊛ Daily noon–midnight

La Lluvia de Oro $

A large bar and restaurant on the north side of Calle Obispo frequented by mixed crowds of Cubans and foreign visitors. The menu, though not elaborate, is extensive and reasonably priced – and it's in English as well as Spanish. Colonial-style fans circle lazily overhead above twin rows of wooden tables. The restaurant is open to the narrow alleys on either side leading off Obispo, though access is restricted by elaborate wooden bolts. The helpful staff serve several varieties of local beer, wine, cocktails and fruit juices. The best deals are the simple but filling combination platters – a choice of fried chicken, pork or fish served with *Moros y Christianos* (black beans and rice) and potato chips for just US$2.50. If you're exploring the Obispo area, this is an excellent place to stop for a break.

➕ 179 F4 ⊠ Calle Obispo 316, La Habana Vieja ☎ (7) 620613 ⊛ Daily 10 am–11.30 pm

La Paella $$

La Paella's proud boast is that it offers the best and most authentic Castilian paella in Cuba. Other popular dishes include barbecued shrimp and lobster. The atmosphere is authentically Spanish – very Costa Brava, with traditional Iberian decor and wooden screens. The service is good, the wine list fairly extensive (though predominantly Spanish and Cuban). The prices are quite high but not unreasonable.

➕ 179 F4 ⊠ Calles Oficios and Obrapia, La Habana Vieja ☎ (7) 671037 ⊛ Daily noon–11

La Terrazza de Cojímar $$

One of Hemingway's most favoured haunts, this is an unpretentious but clean and welcoming seaside restaurant overlooking Cojímar's old Spanish fort. Fronted by a bar-café, the restaurant has 15 red-clothed tables in an airy room featuring numerous framed pictures of "Papa Hemingway". Prices are perhaps a bit high, but you're paying for a little piece of history as well as your meal. The menu is unusually extensive for contemporary Cuba and features seafood. The house speciality – lobsters – are kept live in a tank near a bust of the great man. Other dishes include various combinations of pork, chicken, shrimp, oysters, tuna and ham. There's a good selection of wines featuring Chateau de Rochefort, Rosé de Loire and Pouilly Fumé. Not bad for a seaside village on the eastern outskirts of Havana.

✚ 181 E4 ⊠ Calle Real 161 and Calle Candalería, Cojímar, Habana Este ☎ (7) 939232 ⏲ Daily noon–11

La Torre de Marfil $$

This is one of Havana's more sophisticated Chinese restaurants, yet still not really authentic. Although somewhat more expensive than the Chinese eateries in barrio chino, the Sino-Cuban fare is good and the spring rolls fresh and excellent. As is usually the case in Cuba, criollo food is also on the menu. There is some attempt to provide an appropriate atmosphere, from the Chinese signs out front to the "pagoda seats" at the back of the restaurant. Service is good and friendly.

✚ 179 F4 ⊠ Calle Mercaderes 115, between Calles Obispo and Obrapía, La Habana Vieja ☎ (7) 671038 ⏲ Mon–Fri noon–10, Sat–Sun noon–10:30

La Zaragozana $$

Originally established in 1830, La Zaragozana claims to be the oldest restaurant in Havana. Choices available include both international and criollo cuisine. The extensive menu includes seafood (lobster, prawns, squid and cod) and – unusually for Cuba – brocheta de cordero y ternera (lamb and veal brochettes). Paella Zaragozana is a house speciality. There's a good wine list, with French, Italian and Spanish wines as well as Cuban. Most evenings there's live music and Flamenco dancing at 9:30. Famous people who have eaten here include the writer Federico García Lorca, the boxer Rocky Marciano and – almost inevitably – Ernest Hemingway. It's no coincidence that one of Hemingway's favourite drinking places, El Floridita, is right next door – perhaps drop in here for an iced cocktail before dining at La Zaragozana.

✚ 179 E4 ⊠ Calle Monserrate 352, between Calles Obispo and Obrapía, La Habana Vieja ☎ (7) 8671033 ⏲ Daily 24 hours

Restaurante Hanoi $

Dating from the days when Cuba and Vietnam were close ideological allies of the Soviet Union, this friendly and inexpensive establishment offers an unusual but pleasing criollo version of Vietnamese cuisine.

✚ 179 E3 ⊠ Calles Brasil and Bernaza, La Habana Vieja ⏲ Daily noon–11

Taberna de la Muralla $$

An excellent tavern with its own microbrewery producing satisfyingly cold draught beer. Well-positioned in the southwest corner of Plaza Vieja, with delightful views, it sells beer by the glass or the jug together with a selection of tasty dishes. These range from snacks such as hamburgers and pizzas to bistec de cerdo con papas fritas (pork steak and fries). The walls are mustard-coloured with tall iron pillars supporting the high ceiling and cooling fans stir the torpid air.

✚ 179 F4 ⊠ Calles San Ignacio and Muralla, Plaza Vieja, La Habana Vieja ☎ (7) 8664453 ⏲ Daily 11 am–10 pm

Where to...
Shop

Until recently Socialist Cuba had set its face firmly against both consumerism and private property. The rapid development of tourism over the last decade means that this is changing – especially in Havana. The back streets and narrow alleys of La Habana Vieja are a strange mix of poorly-stocked government peso shops and new, upmarket stores offering imported goods and better quality local produce for non-negotiable US dollar prices. The best streets to explore for shopping include Calle Obispo, Calle O'Reilly and Calle Obrapía. There's also more up-market shopping available in Vedado and Miramar.

Souvenirs

Hard currency shops at hotels and all-in resorts sell items such as dolls, woodcarvings, jewellery, stamps and coins. There's sometimes a good selection of books, but almost all about the Cuban revolution and especially Che Guevara. T-shirts and Che-style berets, often with a red star on the front, are ubiquitous and enduringly popular. In Vedado, try the Habana Libre (▶ 64), in Centro go to the Nacional (▶ 65) and in Miramar the Sierra Maestra at Avenida 1, between Calles 0 and 2. In La Habana Vieja the maze of alleys around Obispo and O'Reilly offer plenty of opportunities for souvenir shopping.

Local Produce

Two of Cuba's finest local products are rum and cigars. These are both generally acknowledged to be among the best, if not the best, in the world. It's better to avoid buying these products from private

traders as you may well find them confiscated at the airport on your departure. Besides, goods sold for hard currency at government shops are tax free and similar in price to goods sold at the duty free airport counters. In Havana cigars and rum are widely available at all government hotels, but don't miss the opportunity to visit the Fábrica de Tabacos Partagás (▶ 60) which sells the best cigars at the end of each tour. Also worthy of note is the excellent local Cuban coffee. Cubita, Turquina and Hola are the top brands and are available at most branches of the hard currency chain Tiendas Panamericanas.

Music

Tapes and, increasingly, compact discs featuring all manner of Cuban music are available throughout Havana. Performers at nightclubs and even on street corners will approach you with copies of their own music, but once again it's probably best to buy through

government outlets. The Cuban State Recording Company, Egrem, produces high quality CDs and cassettes, and you can be sure you are getting the real thing. Musical instruments are also popular souvenirs, from maracas through guitars to violins. For all things musical visit Artex on Calles 23 and L (opposite the Habana Libre Hotel). Also good is the Palacio de la Artesanía in La Habana Vieja at Calle Cuba 64.

Art

Numerous art galleries and street markets in Havana sell paintings, prints and sculptures by local Cuban artists. There's quite a range of styles on show, from Socialist Realism, through Cuban-style Impressionism to Modern Art. Once again, be sure to buy at an approved state outlet and keep the receipt, or you risk having your artwork confiscated by the airport customs. All the squares of La Habana Vieja have art markets, though the best are to be found at the Plaza de la Catedral (Tue–Sun) and in the eastern part of the Old City by the Castillo de la Real Fuerza. There are also art markets at the citadels of El Morro and La Cabaña. More expensive paintings, some by artists of international renown, are found in art shops along La Habana Vieja's Calle Obispo.

Antiques and Second-hand Books

There isn't much of a trade in antiques, as the Cuban authorities are intent on preserving antiquities and their interpretation of what might or might not be a "national treasure" can be pretty random and often severe. Second-hand books are another matter – Cuba is a society which places a high value on literacy, and second-hand book markets can provide some real bargains, though usually in Spanish. The Plaza de Armas in Old Havana is perhaps the best and liveliest sec-

ond-hand book market in the country (closed on Mondays). Most books are in Spanish, but writings in English, French, German and even Russian are also available. There are no fixed prices or government controls here – bargain hard. Also on Plaza de Armas try Librería Bella Habana in the Palacio del Segundo Cabo. Other bookstores worth checking include La Moderna Poesía on Calle Obispo near Parque Central. Directly opposite is La Internacional which sells some titles for pesos and some for dollars, depending on rarity.

Imported Goods

Scarce imported goods such as speciality foods, brand name clothing, toiletries, electronic items, cameras and film are sometimes available at special government stores and can only be purchased with US dollars. In La Habana Vieja the best of these is Harris Brothers behind the Edeficio Bacardí on Calle Zulueta (near the

Plaza Hotel), but despite the store's hard currency status supplies remain very limited. Slide film, in particular, is almost unobtainable, and visitors should ensure they bring an ample supply with them when they enter the country. Beyond La Habana Vieja, the main shopping streets of Centro are Calles Neptuno, San Miguel and San Raphael – not that there's always much for sale on the shelves. In Vedado check out the International Press Centre on the junction of Avenida 23 (La Rampa) and Calle 0 – an oasis for local and foreign newspapers. In Miramar (the relatively affluent embassy district), the large 5 y 42 Complex on Calle 42 and Avenida 5 has stores selling imported luxuries for hard currency shoppers, including a wide selection of speciality food items. Also in Miramar at Avenida 3 and Calle 70, well-stocked Diplotienda, once exclusively for foreign diplomats, is now open to anyone with hard currency.

Hard Currency Food Chains

A new phenomenon which is proving popular with dollar-holding Cubans and can be invaluable to foreign visitors is the government-owned chain Tiendas Panamericanas. Imported foodstuffs, cosmetics, toiletries and drinks are available here, though as ever in Cuba there's no guarantee that shelves, once depleted, will be restocked for weeks at a time. Branches of Tiendas Panamericanas can be found both in Havana and at larger destinations across the country. This is the best and most reliable place to go to stock up on bottled water (both still and gaseous), instant coffee, imported sauces to spice up the often rather bland criollo cuisine, shampoo, toothpaste and many other everyday necessities which are frequently unavailable elsewhere in Cuba. Both US dollars and convertible pesos (▶ 171) are accepted at Tiendas Panamericanas, but ordinary Cuban pesos are not.

Where to...
Be Entertained

Under Socialism Havana might appear to be but a shadow of its former self, yet Habaneros are an inventive lot and insist on having a good time. It would be a mistake to think that the impact of revolutionary morality was purely negative. It's true that the seedier side of pre-revolutionary Havana has been severely circumscribed, but many people would consider this a good thing. It's also true that under Castro the Arts have been encouraged, with classical music, ballet and theatre thriving. Yet some sections of the population, notably gays, have suffered severe persecution, while Carnival – for years discouraged as frivolous – is only just making a comeback. Fortunately, as a result of recent social and economic reforms,

Havana is coming alive again, and the entertainment scene is now as exhilarating as anywhere in the Caribbean.

THE ARTS

Top of the list must be La Habana Vieja's **Gran Teatro** at Paseo de Martí 458 (▶ 60). Regular performances of classical music and ballet are held, and prices are low. A dress code is enforced, however – no shorts or thongs. Classical music and jazz performances are also given at **Teatro Amadeo Roldán** at Avenida 7 and Calle D in Vedado. For avant-garde theatre try **Teatro Mella** at Calles 7 and A, also in Vedado. The **Teatro Nacional** by the Plaza de la Revolución at Paseo and Calle 39 offers classical and

contemporary music performances, theatre and dance. Finally **Teatro Karl Marx** at Calles 7 and A, also in Vedado, features big band performances.

MUSIC AND DANCE

Informal and often spontaneous musical events characterise *Habanero* life. **Cumbanchas** or street parties and **pesas** or jam sessions can occur almost anywhere at almost any time. Mostly information is passed on by word of mouth, but if you're not part of the grapevine, just follow the sounds of *sol, samba, cha-cha-chá and rumba* – you'll be made most welcome. For more formal gatherings, try the **Casa de la Trova** at Centro, Calle San Lázaro 661 (Thursday to Sunday evenings, 7–10 pm). Other venues include **Encounter with Cuban Music** in La Habana Vieja at Calle San Ignacio 78 (Monday and Friday evenings). Caserón del Tango, also in La Habana Vieja at

Calle Justiz 21 (Wednesday and Friday evenings, shows on Saturday evenings). Finally **El Gran Palenque** at 103 Calle 4, Calzada – an Afro-Cuban rumba venue run by the Conjuncto Folklorico Nacional de Cuba (Saturdays, 3–5 pm).

NIGHTLIFE

Havana's nightlife is justifiably legendary. There's a wealth of discos, bars, nightclubs and down-market holes-in-the-wall. At the top end only hard currency holders are able to gain access, but local discos and bars are open to all-and-sundry. The most popular venues are constantly changing, so it makes sense to ask around – your hotel reception desk will have a good idea of what's happening and when. Otherwise, as elsewhere in Havana, follow the beat. Top bars include **La Bodeguita del Medio** at Calle Empedrado 207 and **El Floridita** at Calle Obispo 557, both formerly haunts of Ernest Hemingway and both in La Habana Vieja. Over in Vedado **Bar Turquino** at the Hotel Habana Libre (▶ 64) is enduringly popular, as is the **Jazz Café** at Galerías de Paseo, Calles Paseo and 1 in Vedado – featuring live jazz nightly. Just about every hotel has a bar or sometimes two (one in the lobby and one on the rooftop). As for everyday Cuban bars, it's hardly necessary to list them as they spring up and disappear almost overnight. If you want to walk on the dark side a little bit, try the area between **Parque Central** and **Avenida Italia** – there are numerous small, seedy but authentically atmospheric bars in this area, which is very different to tourist-friendly La Habana Vieja. Keep your hand on your wallet!

DISCOS

Disco Chang at Calle San Nicolas 517, Centro Habana, has loud, pumping music and is frequented by locals as well as visitors. **Macumba Habana** at La Giraldilla,

Calle 222, 37/51 is a popular open-air disco which is often preceded by fashion shows or a cabaret. For rap you might check out **Café Concert Gato Tuerto** at Calle O, 17/19 in Vedado, while for a more tradition-ally Cuban feel the **Cabaret Copa Room** at Hotel Riviera at Paseo and Malecón. **Patio de María** on Calle 37 between Paseo and Calle 2 offers a very Cuban mix of rock music and *salsa*.

CABARET

The casinos and sex shows of pre-revolutionary Havana are long gone, together with the gangsters who ran them (▶ 18). Now Las Vegas-style floorshows rule the roost, mostly featuring scantily-clad dancers with tiny g-strings, elabo-rate head-dresses, feather boas and the like. The most extravagant and opulent of these is the **Cabaret Tropicana** at 4504 Calle 72, Mariano, in the far west of the city (closed Mondays). If you don't want

to go so far out of town, a good alternative is the **Cabaret Parisién** at the Hotel Nacional (▶ 65). There's also an elaborate and colourful cabaret at the **Habana Café** in the Hotel Meliá Cohiba and at the **Salón Turquino** in the Hotel Habana Libre. It's a good idea to book in advance for these shows, especially if you're planning on visiting the Tropicana. Entry prices usually include a first drink. Under the Castro government the shows, though decidedly sexy, are never decadent.

CINEMA

There are over 150 cinemas in Havana, but most are very run down. There are generally two shows a day, at 5 pm and 8 pm. Top of the line is **Cine Payret** at Paseo de Martí 505, opposite the Capitolio. Dating from 1878 this luxurious cinema has five or six screenings a day. In Vedado go to **Cine Yara** at the junction of Calles

23 and L which opens at noon and has six daily screenings.

FESTIVALS

The big event in Havana was once the **Carnaval de la Habana**, formerly celebrated every July along Paseo de Martí and the Malecón. For a couple of decades under the revolution it was considered frivo-lous and counter-revolutionary, but now it's back – only in November, to catch the tourist season. Featuring processions, floats, music and dance, it still seems more stage-managed than the equivalent event in Santiago de Cuba (▶ 137). Other important Havana festivals include the **International Percussion Festival** in April, the **International Guitar Festival** (biennial) in May, the **International Ballet Festival** (biennial) at the **Gran Teatro** in October, and the **New Latin American Film Festival**, held at the Hotel Nacional every December.

Western Cuba

Getting Your Bearings

Although closer to Havana than almost any other part of the country, Western Cuba is relatively isolated and backward. It also differs from the central and eastern plains in that tobacco is the most important crop, not sugar.

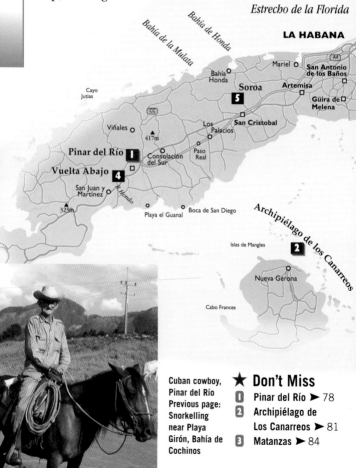

Estrecho de la Florida

LA HABANA

Bahía de Honda

Bahía de la Mulata

Mariel ○ · **San Antonio de los Baños**

Bahía Honda

Soroa [5] · **Artemisa** · **Güira de Melena**

Cayo Jutías

Viñales ○ · CC · 417m · Los Palacios · **San Cristobal**

Pinar del Río [1] · Consolación del Sur · Paso Real

Vuelta Abajo [4]

San Juan y Martínez · R. Hondo · 323m

Playa el Guanal · Boca de San Diego

Archipiélago de los Canarreos

Islas de Mangles [2]

Nueva Gerona

Cabo Francés

Cuban cowboy, Pinar del Río
Previous page: Snorkelling near Playa Girón, Bahía de Cochinos

★ **Don't Miss**

The main link between Havana and Pinar del Río, the chief
city of the west, is the *autopista* (motorway). It's not a long

Wading in the
sea at Varadero

or particularly
arduous
journey, but within a
couple of hours you'll
find you have left
sophisticated
Havana for a town
of horse-drawn
carriages and
moustachioed,
cigar-smoking
guajiros
(peasants).
Beyond Pinar,
with its faded
colonial
architecture,
the west has
much to
offer.
To the
north the
lush hills of
the Sierra del
Rosario shelter a
wide diversity of
wildlife, as well as two
very appealing hill resorts –
Soroa and Las Terrazas. A minor road,
the *circuito norte*, leads back to Havana
via the attractive shores of the Gulf of
Mexico, giving fine views over the
Archipiélago de los Colorados.

Immediately north of Pinar del Río,
the old village and valley of Viñales
(➤ 154) have an enduring appeal
which draws many visitors. To the west
minor roads lead to San Juan y
Martínez and the tobacco centre of
Vuelta Abajo, before winding still further westwards to the town of Punta
María La Gorda.

At Your Leisure

Western Cuba, though relatively close to the capital, Havana, is surprisingly isolated from the mainstream of Cuban life. It's a great place to kick back and relax, with some of the best scenery, watersports and trekking in the country.

Western Cuba in Four Days

Day One

Morning
Drive to Pinar del Río, the cultural and commercial capital of western Cuba, and enjoy lunch at the Hotel Globo.

Afternoon
Spend the afternoon exploring the town of **❶ Pinar del Río** (➤ 78) on foot, perhaps finishing with a *Guayabita del Pinar* at one of the bars on Calle Martí.

Evening/night
It's probably best to retire early – there's no nightlife worth speaking of beyond the Disco Azul at the Hotel Pinar del Río (➤ 91).

Day Two

Morning
Take a taxi or drive to **❹ Vuelta Abajo** (➤ 87), the most famous cigar tobacco-producing district in Cuba and indeed the world.

Afternoon
If you're in a hurry, head back along the *autopista* to Havana. Alternatively drive north from Pinar del Río through the lovely village of Viñales (➤ 154) and take the picturesque but pot-holed *Circuito Norte* (➤ 154) to the mountain resort of Soroa (➤ 87).

Evening/night
Whether you choose to overnight in Havana or Soroa, be ready for an early flight in the morning.

Day Three

Morning
Take a taxi out to Havana Airport and fly to the **2 Archipiélago de los Canarreos** – you can choose between **Nueva Gerona** (➤ 82) or **Cayo Largo** (➤ 82).

Afternoon
Either explore the Special Municipality of the **Isla de la Juventud** (➤ 81), or enjoy some of the best swimming and diving anywhere in the world at **Cayo Largo.**

Evening/night
Fly back to Havana for the night.

Day Four

Morning
Choose from busy **6 Varadero** (➤ 88) or the more isolated **10 Playa Girón** (➤ 90). To get to Varadero, drive east along the northern *autopista* to **3 Matanzas** (➤ 84). For Playa Girón, head south along the *autopista nacional* to the **8 Península de Zapata** (➤ 89).

Afternoon
Either explore the sleepy town of **7 Cárdenas** (➤ 88) with its horse-drawn buses and famous cathedral and Columbus statue (left) before heading back to Varadero, or visit the historic **9 Bahía de Cochinos** (➤ 90) before continuing to Playa Girón.

Evening/night
Check into one of the top-class hotels in **6 Varadero** (➤ 88) or a beach resort at **10 Playa Girón** (➤ 90).

❶ Pinar del Río

Pinar del Río is one of Cuba's largest provinces, taking up much of the western part of the island. It has traditionally been viewed as a rather backward, rural area which, despite its relative proximity to Havana, is "down home" and unsophisticated. The new *autopista* connecting Pinar del Río town with Havana, built by the communist authorities more than 20 years ago, was meant to change all this – but there's little traffic, and Pinar remains a remarkably quiet and laid-back destination.

Pinar del Río is – or rather was – Cuba's "cigar city". The surrounding fertile land is ideally suited to producing tobacco, and during the 19th century the entire region grew relatively prosperous on the strength of this one crop. This wealth explains the many elegant, if faded haciendas and townhouses which still dot the region. It's easy to see that Pinar was once a fairly rich town.

No more. In the late 19th century the major cigar-producing factories moved their operations to nearby Havana, and Pinar del Río lost much of its wealth, becoming an agricultural backwater. Unfortunately, Castro's emphasis on developing agriculture and the countryside has resulted in the fine old colonial buildings falling into serious disrepair – but most are not beyond restoration, and in time, as tourism flourishes, Pinar should once again become a small city of quiet elegance.

Religious image in the Catedral de San Rosendo

Pinar's important sites include the **Museo de Ciencias Naturales** (Museum of Natural Science), also known locally as the **Palacio Guasch**, which houses a collection of stuffed animals, birds and preserved insects from all over the world. It was established by a local doctor, Francisco Guasch, in 1914. A world traveller, he brought back not just preserved insects and wildlife of all kinds, but also an unusual and eclectic taste for various styles of architecture ranging from Gothic, through Moorish to Roman. These are combined in the stucco towers and frontage of the Palacio Guasch, which also houses a collection of concrete dinosaurs in its back garden. The eccentric architecture makes the museum hard to miss.

Rum and Cigar Factories

About 200m (650 yards) south from the town centre intersection of Calle Martí and Isabel Rubio stands a small factory, the **Fábrica de Bebidas Casa Garay**. This is the only distillery in the world producing *Guayabita del Pinar* liquor, often billed as a brandy but in fact a fortified and specially flavoured rum. Distilled rum is brought to the factory and sealed in oak casks together with locally grown, pink-coloured *guayabita* or baby guava. It's 40 per cent proof and sells for around US$4 a bottle – a bargain that is uniquely Pinarese! Guided tours of the factory include liquor tasting – there are sweet and dry varieties – as well as the almost obligatory Cuban attempt to sell you some cigars. Tours are given in Spanish and in English.

Just a couple of hundred metres northwest of the **Catedral de San Rosendo** – Pinar's finest church, built in 1883, and chiefly notable for its stained-glass windows – is

Horse-drawn buggy on Pinar's main street

the **Fábrica de Tabacos Francisco Donatién**, the town's most famous cigar factory. As with the Fábrica de Bebidas, the management are only too pleased to welcome visitors and show them around the establishment. Here you can see workers hand-rolling the cigars (be prepared for a smoky atmosphere – employees are free to smoke as many as they wish) and follow the various processes of cigar production from dried leaf to finished product. Naturally the factory shop will do its best to sell you licensed, legal cigars as part of the tour – the premium brand is Vegueros.

Those with an interest in the 19th-century history of Pinar del Río and the lifestyle of its once-famous tobacco barons should visit the **Museo Provincial de Historia**. This is housed in a colonial mansion and filled with various memorabilia including a contemporaneous dining room with a large, oil-painted landscape of the tobacco fields around Pinar.

Bizarre imagery in the Palacio Guasch

TAKING A BREAK

Try the restaurants in either **Hotel Globo** or **Hotel Pinar del Río**. Cheap pizzas are available at stores along Calle Martí.

✚ 180 C3
Museo de Ciencias Naturales
✉ Calle Martí 202
☎ (82) 3087
🕐 Tue–Sat 9–4:30, Sat 8–11:30am
💷 Inexpensive

Fábrica de Bebidas Casa Garay
✉ Calle Isabel Rubio 189

☎ (82) 2966
🕐 Mon–Fri 8:30–4:30
💷 Inexpensive

Fábrica de Tabacos Francisco Donatién
✉ Calle Antonio Maceo 157
☎ (82) 3424
🕐 Mon–Fri 7:30–4:30, Sat 7:30–11:30am
💷 Moderate

PINAR DEL RÍO: INSIDE INFO

Top tip Take a **horse carriage** round town for an authentic feel of this antiquated and isolated town.

One to miss Watch out for hustlers who will try to sell you **illegal (unlicensed) cigars** which will be confiscated at Havana airport.

② Archipiélago de Los Canarreos

Although strictly speaking the chain of islands that makes up the Archipiélago de Los Canarreos is part of Western Cuba, it's geographically quite different, being separated from the mainland by the 100km (62 miles) wide Golfo de Batabanó, and only accessible by air from Havana or by ferry from Surgidero de Batabanó in Havana Province.

The archipelago itself is not well served with communications. If you wish to travel from the larger Isla de la Juventud in the west to the popular beach resorts of Cayo Largo del Sur in the east, you will either have to charter a boat or return to Havana to board a new flight. The ferry service from Surgidero de Batabanó cannot be recommended – it may be relatively cheap, but it's slow, crowded and unreliable.

The main island in the archipelago, long known as the "Island of Pines" and now as the **Isla de la Juventud**, is where most Cubans live and least tourists stay. Known colloquially as "La Isla", its isolation means it has long been used for a variety of nefarious activities, and was once known to British privateers as "Parrot Island", a hiding place from official authorities.

Later it became infamous as the site of the **Presidio Modelo**, a harsh isolation prison used to incarcerate political detainees, as well as some of Cuba's more dangerous criminals. Fidel Castro was held here for for some months after his attack on the Moncada Barracks in 1953. The Presidio Modelo is often described in tourist literature as the island's most interesting site. However the great, circular prison towers (although long since disused) are depressing rather than uplifting, and most visitors to the archipelago choose the beaches and dive sites of Cayo Largo as an alternative.

Catamaran off Cayo Largo

The Main Town

The capital of Isla de la Juventud, **Nueva Gerona**, is a pleasant place. Founded in 1830, its chief exports are citrus fruits and marble. The main church, **Iglesia Nuestra Señora de los Dolores**, overlooks **Parque Julio Antonio Mella**, the town's central square. It's a somnolent place, without a great deal to see apart from the **Museo de la Lucha Clandestina** (Museum of the Clandestine Struggle). Southwest of town you will find the **Museo Finca El Abra**, a farmhouse-turned-museum where José Martí, the great Cuban patriot, was held under house arrest for three months in the late 19th century.

It's not the bucolic charm of Nueva Gerona that draws foreign visitors to "La Isla", but the numerous dive sites off the **Costa de los Piratas** (Pirate Coast). This area, reputedly filled with the wrecks of sunken Spanish galleons and English and Dutch pirate vessels, dominates the large bay known as **Bahía Siguanea** off the west coast of the island. A number of Spanish and other wrecks are preserved in reasonable condition in the warm waters of the bay, teeming with fish and easily accessible to trained divers. Here, too, is the **Caribbean Cathedral**, supposedly the tallest living coral column anywhere in the world.

Isolated Islands

Cayo Largo is the largest of the small group of keys which make up the eastern half of the Archipiélago de los Canarreos. Just 24km (15 miles) long and shaped like a sickle moon, Cayo Largo is 200km (124 miles) southeast of Havana and more than

Above: Kayaking at Cayo Largo
Lef: Bananas heading for market in Nueva Gerona

100km (62 miles) east of the Isla de la Juventud. It's dedicated to international tourism and you won't find many Cubans here unless they're working in the service industry or rich expatriates on holiday from the United States.

Cayo Largo is indeed spectacular. If you're looking for a Robinson Crusoe paradise Cayo Largo is probably the place. The only activities are wining, dining, sunbathing and – above all – swimming, snorkelling and diving. There's even a nudist beach at Playa Blanca (most unusual for puritanical Cuba where topless bathing is frowned upon). It's also possible to charter private boats for trips to other, nearby deserted keys – and scuba diving courses are available. This is a great place for a complete break away from it all, but there's almost nothing genuinely Cuban about Cayo Largo.

TAKING A BREAK

For something a little different try **Restaurante El Dragón** at Calle 39 in Nueva Gerona – it's Chinese.

✚ 181 D3
Presidio Modelo
✉ 4km (2.5 miles) east of Nueva Gerona at Reparto Chacón
☎ (61) 25112
🕐 Tue–Sun 8–4
💵 Inexpensive

Museo de la Lucha Clandestina
✉ Calles 24 and 45
☎ (61) 24582
🕐 Tue–Sat 9–5, Sun 8–noon
💵 Inexpensive

Museo Finca El Abra
✉ 3km (1.8 miles) southwest of Nueva Gerona
🕐 Tue–Sun 9–5
💵 Inexpensive

ARCHIPIÉLAGO DE LOS CANARREOS: INSIDE INFO

Top tips Don't try and bring cigars from Nueva Gerona to the mainland unless you have an authentic certificate of government sale. The customs authorities between the archipelago and the mainland have a reputation for being thorough.

• If you're in Nueva Gerona anytime between October and March try to catch a baseball game at the **Estadio Cristóbal Labra**.

• A great way to explore Nueva Gerona and around is by horse cart or *carretone*. These are available for hire by the **Cubalse Supermarket** on Calle 35 for around US$10 per day including driver.

❸ Matanzas

Matanzas is sometimes referred to as the "Athens of Cuba" because of its architecture and literary traditions. It was once a major exporter of livestock to Spain and remains a relatively prosperous port city, with a number of impressive churches and civic buildings.

The coast road east from Havana runs past a series of attractive beaches known as the **Playas del Este** before entering Matanzas Province at the remarkable **Mirador de Bacunayagua**, a raised viewpoint overlooking Cuba's highest (110m, 360 feet) and longest (314m, 1,030 feet) bridge, spanning a deep ravine which separates the two provinces. There's a petrol station and a restaurant here, on a small hill to the left (north) of the road. It's worth stopping to fill up the tank, have a cool drink, and gaze down into the ravine which is lined with royal palms and usually filled with wheeling turkey buzzards sailing on the wind.

An Ancient Entrepot
Matanzas is a medium-sized port city with a population of around 130,000. It grew wealthy in the

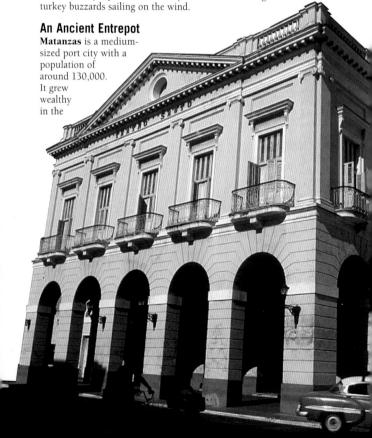

The altar and nave of the neo-classical Iglesia de San Pedro Apóstol

17th and 18th centuries as an importer of slaves and an exporter of livestock. Its real heyday came in the 19th century, however, when sugar and coffee began to be exported from the excellent, sheltered Bahía de Matanzas in bulk. In 1843 the railway from Havana reached the town, and Matanzas became, briefly, Cuba's second city.

The historic heart of Old Matanzas dates from this time, and it is here that most of the worthwhile sites are found. It's not a large area, located between the Río Yumurí to the north and the Río San Juan to the south, and can be explored comfortably on foot in about an hour.

The centre of Matanzas is **Plaza de la Vigía**, and this is a good place to start an exploration of the city. In the middle of the square is a statue dedicated to the Cuban independence hero **Antonio Maceo**, while just across from this the neo-classical **Parque de los Bomberos**, built in 1897, still houses the city's fire brigade. On the opposite side of the square is the **Galería de Arte Provincial**, while facing the art gallery is the neo-classical **Teatro Sauto** (1862), with marble statues of Greek goddesses standing in the entrance hall – maybe this is where the "Athens of Cuba" nickname comes from?

Either way, it's the feel of the Plaza de la Vigía rather than any of the particular buildings which give this part of central Matanzas its special atmosphere.

Next door to the Provincial Art Gallery is the **Ediciones Vigía**, a real craftsman's factory producing hand-bound, first-edition books in runs of just 200 copies. You can watch them being made – they are

Left: The imposing façade of Teatro Sauto

real works of art – and perhaps purchase a copy as a souvenir for around US$10 a volume.

The Ecclesiastical Core

To the west, behind Plaza de la Vigía, a series of narrow streets lined with some attractive colonnaded buildings leads for several hundred metres into the heart of the old city. Here you will find the **Catedral de San Carlos Borromeo**, one of the city's finest buildings. Originally constructed in 1693, it was restored in the mid-19th century. Unfortunately it's in serious need of further renovation. Close by is **Parque Libertad**, with a statue to the national hero José Martí and the great iron wheel of an old *ingenio*, or sugar mill.

Garlic sellers on the road near Matanzas

The south side of Parque Libertad is home to another of Matanzas' unusual institutions, the **Museo Farmacéutico** which dates from the 1880s. Today this fine old traditional pharmacy has been preserved as a museum, complete with its original ceramic and glass medicine jars, hardwood cabinets and medicinal prescriptions.

Away from the town centre, in the more northerly district of Versalles, the old church known as **Iglesia de San Pedro Apóstol** is worth visiting. In better condition than the cathedral, it has some fine stained-glass windows and good views south over Matanzas Harbour.

TAKING A BREAK

There are a few cheap local restaurants serving sandwiches scattered here and there, but the best place in town is the **Café Atenas** on Plaza de la Vigía which serves spaghetti and pizza.

➕ 181 F4
Galería de Arte Provincial
✉ Calle 272, Plaza de la Vigía
🕐 Mon–Sat 9–6
💲 Inexpensive

Ediciones Vigía
✉ Calle 272, Plaza de la Vigía

🕐 Mon–Fri 9–4
💲 Inexpensive

Museo Farmacéutico
✉ Calle 83 Milanés 4951
🕐 Mon–Sat 10–6, Sun 9–1
💲 Inexpensive

MATANZAS: INSIDE INFO

Top tips Visit Matanzas as a day trip from either Havana or Varadero, or better still en route from Havana to Varadero. It's a good place to break your journey and **have a snack**.

• Between 10 and 20 October every year the **Festival del Bailador Rumbero** is held at Matanzas' Teatro Sauto.

At Your Leisure

4 Vuelta Abajo

Cuba is well-known as the source of the world's finest cigars, and it has long been acknowledged that the very finest cigar tobacco comes from the district of Vuelta Abajo. This fertile valley located around the small town of San Juan y Martínez, just cloth from direct sunlight, while tobacco-drying sheds where leaves are hung to cure can be seen everywhere.

➕ 180 B3

5 Soroa

Soroa is a lush hill resort in the hills

The Vale of Soroa

22km (13.6 miles) southwest of Pinar del Río, is well worth a half-day's visit – after all, Cuba still exports around 100 million cigars annually, worth an estimated US$50 million in imports. The secret of Vuelta Abajo lies in the unusual richness of the red soil, which is well-watered but (crucially) quite dry during the tobacco growing season. The local peasant farmers are friendly and used to showing people around – though a tip is usually expected.

Green fields of tobacco leaves cover the region, many protected by of the Sierra del Rosario just 75km (46.5 miles) southwest of Havana. It's close enough to the capital to make an ideal weekend retreat, and during the early years of the Cuban Revolution it was much favoured by the communist élite. Today – especially now that Fidel has decreed that "tourism is gold" – it serves a wider clientele. The main resort, Villa Soroa, offers luxurious individual villas, an excellent swimming pool and one of the best buffet dinners in Cuba. High in the hills above is another restaurant, El Castillo de las Nubes (The Castle in the Clouds). There's also a fine orchid garden with over 300 species on display, but the

The Catedral de la Immaculada
Concepción, Cárdenas

most popular sight is the **Salto del Arco Iris**, an attractive waterfall with a cool swimming area beneath, which is popular with visitors. Be warned, though – after violent rains the falls become dangerously powerful, and swimming is not recommended.

✚ 181 D4
Salto del Arco Iris
💲 Moderate, free if you stay at Villa Soroa

6 Varadero

Varadero – more precisely the long and narrow Punta Hicacos Peninsula – is Cuba's primary tourist resort and the nearest thing that you'll find to Spain's Costa del Sol. The entire peninsula is given over to tourism, with most hotels specialising in "all-in" packages or tourist flights direct from Europe and Canada to the international airport, just 6km (3.7 miles) off the main highway between Matanzas and Varadero.

Varadero has its good points and its bad, but it's certainly not the real Cuba. Most Cubans are forbidden access to the peninsula unless they have employment there. Payments are universally in US$ dollars or – a sign of the times – euros. Most types of watersport are available, and the seas are warm, safe and clean. Skydiving is a popular activity. The food is some of the best in Cuba – served mostly as buffet lunches and dinners in all-in resorts. If you're on a two-week package to escape the European winter and soak up the sun, it may be the best place on the island.

✚ 182 A5 ✈ Juan Gualberto Gómez Internacional Airport

7 Cárdenas

If you're staying in Varadero and want to experience the real Cuba,

then Cárdenas is the easiest and most natural place to go. Just 18km (11 miles) southeast of Varadero along a good (if narrow) highway, it's quintessentially Cuban. There's not much to the town, which has a population of about 75,000 inhabitants, many of whom seem to be under-employed if not unemployed. There's an old, run-down shipyard, a rum factory and the usual sugar mills in the surrounding countryside.

But Cárdenas *does* have atmosphere. Built on an easy-to-follow grid pattern, the town is centred on the Catedral de la Immaculada Concepción (c. 1850), a fine old church noted for its stained-glass windows and fronted by a statue of Christopher Columbus sculpted by the Spanish artist Piquier in 1862. There's also an unusual cast-iron market called Plaza Molocoff dating from 1859 with a 16m (52.5ft)-high dome which is

worth taking a look at. Cárdenas is known for the rows of colonnaded, single storey private houses, mostly painted in pale, faded pastels, and the elaborate iron grilles guarding the windows. The whole town seems to run on horse or donkey power, and there is very little in the way of places to eat or stay. It is, however, an excellent and highly contrasting day trip from Varadero.

➕ 182 A5

8 Península de Zapata

Most of southern Matanzas Province is given over to the sugar fields, swamps and the badlands of the Zapata Peninsula. There are no large towns, and the only major road – the *autopista* from Havana to Santa Clara – runs from west to east, not north to south. Take a right turn down the minor road at Jagüey Grande, almost in the middle of Matanzas Province, and you'll be heading right into the heart of Zapata.

Most of the 4,500sq km (1,755sq miles) peninsula is now included in the Grand Parque Natural Montemar, and is an obvious destination for birdwatchers and nature lovers of all kinds. It's also one of the few places where you will have a good chance of seeing a Cuban manatee or sea cow. Nature aside, Zapata is also the

Relaxing at Playa Girón

location of the "Bay of Pigs" (➤ below), site of the CIA-sponsored Cuban mercenary invasion defeated by Castro in 1961. Just south of Jagüey Grande, at a vast sugar mill called Central Australia, the **Museo de la Comandancia** commemorates these events and is worth a visit.

About 18km (11 miles) south of Central Australia an Indian village supposedly modelled on the habitations and lifestyles of the pre-Columbian Taíno Indians has been re-created. The 20-minute boat trip through the Zapata marshes to La Boca de Guamá is well worthwhile, both for the wildlife including crocodiles, flamingos and ibis, and for a rare chance to learn something, however spurious, about Cuba's original indigenous population.

The Bahía de Cochinos

✚ 181 F3
Museo de la Comandancia
✉ 2km (1.2 miles) south of Jagüey Grande ◷ Tue–Sat 8–5, Sun 8–noon
📻 Inexpensive

La Boca de Guamá
✉ 18km (11 miles) south of Jagüey Grande 🚢 40-minute roundtrip through the Laguna del Tesoro 📻 Moderate

❾ Bahía de Cochinos

From La Boca the road continues south to the Bahía de Cochinos (Bay of Pigs), site of the infamous CIA invasion. Just why the US intelligence services and their Cuban allies should have decided on this bay as a landing place remains obscure – it's a long way from anywhere of importance, easily isolated, and surrounded by very difficult, marshy countryside. Today the Bay of Pigs is an area of natural beauty, a gorgeous bay opening onto the Caribbean Sea.

At the head of the bay the road divides west to Playa Larga and Las Salinas Wildlife Refuge, famous for the tens of thousands of pink flamingos that congregate there between October and April. To the east, the road follows the shore of the bay past numerous good diving and snorkelling points, the best of which is Cueva de Los Peces, a well-sign-

posted *cenote* or flooded fault in the earth's surface that is more than 70m (230ft) deep. Isolated, cool and with a restaurant next door, it's an excellent place for a break and a meal. The snorkelling in the nearby sea is also highly recommended.

✚ 182 A4

❿ Playa Girón

Beyond Cueva de los Peces the road swings east, still hugging the coast, to reach the isolated resort of Playa Girón. There's a beautiful if largely deserted beach – perhaps the fact that the Bay of Pigs mercenaries landed at this spot in 1961 has kept it sacrosanct, at least for the present, as far as tourism is concerned. There's good snorkelling and swimming, as well as the Museo de Girón, displaying two rooms of photographs and trophies commemorating Castro's triumph over the invaders.

If you're staying in this area, it's better to press on a further 8km (5 miles) to Caleta Buena, a fine dive site with reasonable food and accommodation at Villa Playa Girón. Here there's an International Scuba Centre which specialises in guiding divers through a series of underwater caves populated with sightless fish.

✚ 182 A3
Museo de Girón
✉ Opposite Villa Playa Girón, Playa Girón ◷ Daily 9–noon, 1–6
📻 Moderate

Where to... Stay

Prices
Expect to pay per double room per night
$ under US$50 $$ US$50–150 $$$ over US$150

MATANZAS

El Louvre $

There's no real reason to stay in Matanzas, as better accommodation is readily available in nearby Varadero or slightly more distant Havana. If, however, you need to overnight in the city, then El Louvre is the best option. Situated in the centre of town on the south side of Parque Libertad, facilities include colonial-style bedrooms, an attractive courtyard and a friendly bar. Unlike Varadero, Matanzas sees few visitors who stay overnight, so this is a good place to meet locals.

➕ 181 F4 ⬛ Parque Libertad, Calles 83 and 282 ☎ (52) 4074

NUEVA GERONA

Villa Gaviota $

Probably the best hotel – certainly the most congenial – in Nueva Gerona, Villa Gaviota is near the airport and has fine views across the island, especially at sunset. The staff are friendly, there's a good *criollo* restaurant and there are mini-fridges in the rooms (Nueva Gerona can get pretty humid in summer). However, loud music often blasts from the swimming pool area until well into the evening, particularly at weekends – not that this is in any way unusual for up-country Cuba, where having a good time usually means music and dancing. If you're not into disco, ask for a room well away from the pool.

➕ 181 D3 ⬛ Autopista Nueva Gerona-Santa Fe Km1 ☎ (61) 23290

PINAR DEL RÍO

Pinar del Río $

Though typical of the Soviet-style "leading hotel" to be found on the outskirts of most Cuban provincial capitals, this rather ugly four-storey block remains, nonetheless, the most comfortable and best-appointed accommodation in Pinar del Río. Amenities include 24-hour medical service, several shops, two restaurants and internet services, though the latter are generally not working. There's a large swimming pool, and car rental facilities are available in the lobby. It's ideally located both for the *autopista* and for a walk into town.

➕ 180 C3 ⬛ Calle Martí and Autopista ☎ (82) 5070/75; fax: (82) 5662

PLAYA GIRÓN

Villa Playa Girón $

The largest hotel and bungalow accommodation in Playa Girón, with nearly 300 rooms divided between two larger buildings (30 rooms) and numerous individual bungalows. Facilities include a swimming pool, bar, disco and business centre. The restaurant is large and designed to cater for tour groups. When groups are resident there's a good buffet spread provided, but if only independent travellers are staying, then it's usually à la carte *criollo* specialities. The hotel is right by the beautiful Bay of Pigs, so try the seafood, which is usually excellent and doesn't come any fresher. Even though the sea is literally a stone's throw away, better swimming and snorkelling facilities are available 8km to the southeast at Caleta Buena. This is a picture-perfect beach and cove with scuba centre, small boats available for hire, and a restaurant serving fine alfresco buffet lunches.

➕ 182 A3 ✉ Playa Girón, Bahía de Cochinos, Peninsula de Zapata
☎ (59) 4118; fax: (59) 4117

Villa Soroa $$

This is one of the best and most attractive up-country hotels in Cuba. Set in the hills above Candelaria, accommodation consists of beautiful and well-appointed private bungalows overlooking a fine swimming pool with sunbathing facilities and poolside bar. The related **Castillo de las Nubes** (▶ 87) dominates the nearby hilltop and offers an alternative venue for lunch, though the Villa Soroa restaurant has an excellent *criollo* and international buffet in the evenings which is as varied and tasty as any outside Havana. Staying here entitles guests to free entry to the nearby orchidareum, as well as the Salto del Arco Iris water-

fall. Friendly staff speak English and there's an English menu at the main restaurant.

➕ 181 D4 ✉ Carretera de Soroa Km8, Candelaria ☎ (82) 2122/2041; fax: (82) 802961

Dos Mares $

A reasonably priced, clean and attractive hotel just 100m from the beach with well-appointed rooms, a good bar and an attached seafood restaurant. Dos Mares offers good value and great access both to the sea and to nearby restaurants and night spots. The service can be a bit cool, however. There's an unguarded but convenient car park on Calle 53 outside the main entrance. Prices include breakfast in the next-door restaurant – which is under the same ownership – and the unlimited coffee and fresh fruit are a bonus.

➕ 182 A5 ✉ Avenida 1 and Calle 53
☎ (5) 662702; fax: (5) 667499

Internacional $$$

A long-standing Varadero favourite, this hotel first opened in 1950 as a twin to Miami's Hotel Fontainbleau and has since been restored. It's set right on the beach, with fine views from the top floors. A range of services is provided, swimming pool and tennis courts, Cabaret and Disco Continental, numerous bars and two restaurants, both serving good international and *criollo* fare. The Cafeteria Panorama, close by the beach, has the better atmosphere of the two though the menu is essentially similar. Car rental services and money exchange facilities can be found in the main lobby. English is well spoken by the desk staff, and all menus are in English as well as Spanish.

➕ 182 A5 ✉ Avenida Las Ameritas
☎ (5) 667380; fax: (5) 667246

Pullman $$

Close by – and similar to – the Hotel Dos Mares, the Pullman is one of the better deals in the

medium price range at Varadero. With only 15 rooms it's advisable to book in advance, as it's a long-established favourite with independent travellers. The surroundings are intimate, the ambience Spanish, and the beach about 150m away. Apart from breakfast, it's probably better to eat elsewhere, there are several reasonable restaurants and cafeterias in the vicinity. Parking on the road outside is limited, but across the street near the Hotel Dos Mares spaces should be vacant.

➕ 182 A5 ✉ Avenida 1, Calles 49 and 50 ☎ (5) 667161; fax: (5) 667495

Sol Palmeras $$$

Very much at the top end of the Varadero price range, this huge hotel is a joint venture between Cubanacan and the giant Spanish Sol Mélia chain. The foreign management certainly shows, as service is well above average. There are more than 400 rooms and 20 bungalows arranged around a large swimming pool close by the beach.

Where to...
Eat and Drink

Prices

Expect to pay per person for a two-course meal, excluding drinks and service
$ under US$10   **$$** US$10–25   **$$$** over US$25

Amenities include numerous bars, restaurants, money exchange, pharmacy, car rentals and tennis courts. The choice of food available is unusually extensive for Cuba, with international and Italian cuisine topping the menu. There's a rudimentary business centre, and email services are generally available.

✚ 182 A5 ☒ Carretera de las Morlas, Autopista Sur Km9, Varadero
☎ (5) 667009; fax: (5) 667008

VIÑALES

La Ermita $$

Viñales' best, La Ermita is about 2km east of the small town on a hilltop with fine views. Facilities offered include tennis, swimming and horse-riding. The restaurant provides simple but good food, and the hotel is within walking distance of Viñales' main street and numerous other eateries. The view across Viñales Valley is breathtaking.

✚ 180 C4 ☒ Carretera a La Ermita Km1.5
☎ (8) 936250; fax: (8) 936069

NUEVA GERONA

El Dragon $

This establishment specialises in Chinese cuisine – though the choice is limited and not very sophisticated. Nevertheless, it's reasonably priced, clean and the food is filling – and it's a welcome change to find the (usually excellent) Cuban pork prepared in a "sweet and sour" sauce rather than just grilled, fried or stewed. Staff strike a gong as you enter, and there's music – Cuban, not Chinese – after 7:30 in the evenings. Other Cuban-Chinese dishes on the menu (but not necessarily always available) include chop suey and spring rolls. There are also numerous *criollo* staples – but the décor seems authentically Chinese, at least by Nueva Gerona standards.

✚ 181 D3 ☒ Calles 39 and 26
☎ (61) 24479 ⊕ Tue–Sun noon–10

PINAR DEL RÍO

Rumayor $$

Pinar del Río's main government restaurant is 1km north of town, just off the road to Viñales. It serves quality *criollo* fare as well as a couple of more unusual dishes,

pollo ahumado (smoked chicken) and *caldosa puerco* (stewed pork). The latter is relatively hard to find on up-country menus, but with *Moros y Christianos* (black beans and rice), it's nourishing and tasty. Rumayor often has a nightly cabaret show in a large outdoor amphitheatre featuring especially Cuba's Afro-Caribbean dance and music. Showtime is usually 10 pm, but it's best to check with the management. Admission costs an extra US$5, but the ticket comes with one free drink.

✚ 180 C3 ☒ Carretera Pinar del Río-Viñales Km1 ☎ (82) 63007
⊕ Daily noon–midnight

SOROA

El Castillo de las Nubes $

Set high on Loma del Fuerte, the hill which dominates Soroa, this "Castle in the Clouds" has the feel of a rather dilapidated folly which looks better from a distance than it does close-up. Nevertheless it's an excellent place for a cool drink and a meal, with fine views down into the Soroa Valley and also away south towards the *Autopista Nacional*. The "castle" was built in 1942 by an affluent eccentric called Don Pedro. The latter's residence, now abandoned, stands behind the folly and offers a fine panorama over the southern coastal plain.

➕ 181 D4 ⊠ Loma del Fuerte, Candelaria ☎ (82) 2122/2041 🕑 Daily 10–5

Restaurante Villa Soroa $$

Soroa is more of a hill resort than a town, so there isn't a great deal of choice in places to eat. In fact, there's really only one worth considering, and that's the restaurant attached to the Villa Soroa (▶ 87). It's unusually good for a Cuban government-run hotel, offering a really exceptional buffet which includes a wide selection of *criollo* pork, chicken and beef dishes, local soups, salads and desserts such as crème caramel and cream cake in addition to fresh sliced pineapple and water melon. There's a reasonable wine list, too – perhaps reflecting the fact that Villa Soroa has served for many years as a retreat for the Cuban communist elite.

➕ 181 D4 ⊠ Carretera de Soroa Km8, Candelaria ☎ (82) 2122/2041; fax: (82) 802961 🕑 Daily 7 am–11 pm

VARADERO

Barracuda Grill $$

Set in a pavilion thatched with nipa palm, right by the beach in the grounds of the Barracuda Diving Centre, this is a great place for barbecued seafood such as shark steaks, prawns, squid and lobster, and even sometimes barracuda. Other items include grilled pork, chicken and beef. The emphasis is very much on grilled or fried food, usually accompanied by *papas fritas* – fried potatoes. Delightful sunsets, cold beer, friendly staff and excellent service.

➕ 182 A5 ⊠ Calle 58 and Avenida 1 ☎ (5) 613481 🕑 Daily 10:30 am–11 pm

El Bodegon Criollo $$

The name tells the story – *criollo* cuisine, but in this case unusually well prepared and more varied than most. Seafood is, understandably, the house speciality, and the lobster is as fresh as one could wish for and quite excellent. The flame-grilled, succulent burgers are pretty good and the bread rolls are soft and palatable, unusual for Cuba where the bread is often hard. If you like your burgers spicy, bring your own *salsa* – jars are readily available in most Varadero supermarkets, but for some reason don't often appear on dining tables.

➕ 182 A5 ⊠ Avenida de la Playa and Calle 40 ☎ (5) 667784 🕑 Daily noon–midnight

Lai Lai $$

Another of Cuba's Chinese restaurants, the cuisine is inevitably partly *criollo* – though because this is Varadero rather than just any provincial town, the choice of dishes is more authentic and more varied than in most Sino-Cuban places. The ambience is studiously Chinese (though the oriental characters on the entrance doors are artistic licence, and not authentically Chinese script). You can choose between sitting at tables or dining cross-legged on the floor. Shuts early for Varadero, so don't leave it too late.

➕ 182 A5 ⊠ Avenida 1A and Calle 18 ☎ (5) 613297 🕑 Daily noon–10:45

El Meson del Quijote $$

Up-market says it all. You can tell this just by looking at the restaurant, which is set in a castle-like tower on top of a low mound by the Carretera La Américas – just look for the metallic statues of Don Quixote, Sancho Panza and their donkey. The cuisine is appropriately Andalusian, and there's a very reasonable wine list featuring, especially, Spanish wines. El Meson is popular, so reservations are recommended.

🏠 182 A5 ☒ Carretera La Américas and Calle B Las Morlas ☎ (5) 613522 🕑 Daily noon–midnight

VIÑALES

La Casa de Don Tomás $$

Perhaps Viñales' best government restaurant, set in an old colonial mansion with character and an outside balcony for alfresco dining. The dish to look out for is called "las delicias de Don Tomás" and consists of a selection of lobster, fish, pork, chicken and sausage served with arroz blanco (white rice), or the ever-popular Moros y Christianos (black beans with rice). Other fare on offer includes fried chicken and pork steaks, various seafood dishes sometimes including fresh lobster, papas fritas and chilled Cuban beer.

🏠 180 C4 ☒ Salvador Cisneros 140 ☎ (8) 936300 🕑 Daily 10 am–10 pm

Where to...
Shop

Despite its proximity to the capital, Cuba west of Havana has few shopping opportunities apart from cigars and rum. The provincial capital, Pinar del Río, is a small town fallen on hard times. That it was once prosperous is obvious from the 19th-century architecture and the local museums (▶ 156), but there's an almost complete lack of hard currency stores and even peso shops are unusually poorly stocked. By contrast, east of Havana Matanzas is relatively well-stocked, while Varadero positively overflows with goods.

Cigars

It's generally agreed that the Pinar del Río district of **Vuelta Abajo** (▶ 87) grows the finest cigar tobacco in the world, and no visi-

tor to Pinar should miss the **Fábrica de Tabacos Francisco Donatién** (▶ 80) where cigars of unusual excellence are for sale.

Rum

Pinar has its own unique rum, *Guayabita del Pinar*, which is found nowhere else in the world and makes a distinctive and reasonably priced souvenir. It's for sale at the **Fábrica de Bebidas Casa Garay** (▶ 79), and is really delicious. There are two varieties, dry and sweet, and both are rated at around 40 per cent alcohol.

Souvenirs

In the west, better to forget Pinar del Río and move on to nearby **Viñales**. Here the main street, especially the square by the **Iglesia Viñales**, has many souvenir stalls selling all manner of knick-knacks, T-shirts and revolutionary memorabilia.

There are several similar outlets in the isolated **Archipiélago de los**

Canarreos, especially at **Nueva Gerona** and **Cayo Largo**. Both these popular destinations also have dive shops and government owned outlets at the major hotels selling suntan lotion, goggles, flippers and the varied apparatus of simple watersports. In Nueva Gerona try the **Villa Gaviota** (▶ 91) or, out on the **Bahía Siguanea**, the **El Colony**.

At **Cayo Largo** there's a string of luxury hotels including **Pelicano**, **Villa Coral**, **Isla del Sur**, **Villa Iguana** and **Villa Capricho**, all located in the southern part of the island.

For a real souvenir shopping spree, however, you can't beat the major malls and tourist hotels of Varadero, which occur every few hundred yards and are impossible to miss. Note that **Varadero** is not just a US dollar zone, but also accepts euros.

In **Matanzas** be sure to watch for the hand-crafted books at **Ediciones Vigía** (▶ 85).

Where to...
Be Entertained

Western Cuba (beyond the City of Havana) can really be divided into three distinct entertainment zones – Varadero, the Archipiélago de los Canarreos, and the rest. In the far west Pinar del Río Province has almost nothing in the way of nightlife or cabarets, and the same is true of Havana Province and nearly all of Matanzas. In Varadero, by contrast, nightlife abounds while both Varadero and Archipiélago de los Canarreos are all about watersports.

The Arts

The Arts in Pinar del Río are represented by the **Teatro José Jacinto Milanés**, a fine old institution featuring weekly musical recitals and theatrical productions, and by the **Casa de la Musica** on Calle Gerardo Medina which stages *punta campesina* folkloric dances.

In Matanzas the **Teatro Sala José White** on Calle 79 presents regular classical concerts and jazz evenings. The better-known **Teatro Sauto** on the Plaza de la Vigía (▶ 85) holds classical concerts on Friday to Sunday evenings. There's a **Casa de la Cultura** at Calle 272 which organises poetry readings and theatrical shows.

In the Archipiélago de los Canarreos there's a **Casa de la Cultura** at **Nueva Gerona** Calle 37.

Nightlife

In Pinar del Río try **La Esquinita Coctelería** on Calle Isabel Rubio Norte for a drink with the locals. In Matanzas the **Ruinas de Matasiete** by the mouth of the Río San Juan is a colourful bar named after a local bandit. In Nueva Gerona try **Casa de los Vinos** at Calle 41. In Cayo Largo del Sur almost all nightlife revolves around the big all-in hotels with plenty of bars and nightclubs.

Discos

The only disco in Pinar del Río is **Disco Azul** at Hotel Pinar (closed Mondays). Matanzas has no disco, but try the **Bar Karaoke** on Calle 298. In Nueva Gerona the top disco is **La Movida** on Calle 18 by the river. Varadero fairly overflows with discos and dance clubs – try **Discoteca La Bamba** at Hotel Tuxpan, Avenida Las Américas.

Cabaret

In Pinar del Río there's a cabaret at **Rumayor** (▶ 93). Matanzas boasts an open-air spectacular, the **Cabaret Tropicana**, at Calle 72 and Línea del Ferrocarril. Nueva Gerona's **Cabaret el Patio** on Calle 24 is open Thursday to Sunday. There are around 10 cabarets in Varadero, the largest of which is **Cabaret Continental** at the Hotel Internacional.

Sports

In Nueva Gerona the **Club de Parapente** at 4304 Calle 16 organises paragliding. Scuba diving can be arranged by **Puertosol International Diving Center** at the Hotel El Colony on the Ensenada de la Siguanea.

On Cayo Largo del Sur the various all-in hotels offer a wide range of watersports, and there's a **dive shop** at Playa Sirena. For fuller details go to www.cubajunky.com/-isla-juventud/index.

Varadero offers a wide range of snorkelling, scuba diving, windsurfing, sailing, kayaking, deep-sea fishing and even skydiving. Contact the **Centro de Información Turística Rumbos** on Avenida 1 at Calle 23. For further details of everything Varadero has to offer, go to www.cubajunky.com/matanzas/-varadero-home.

Central Cuba

Getting Your Bearings

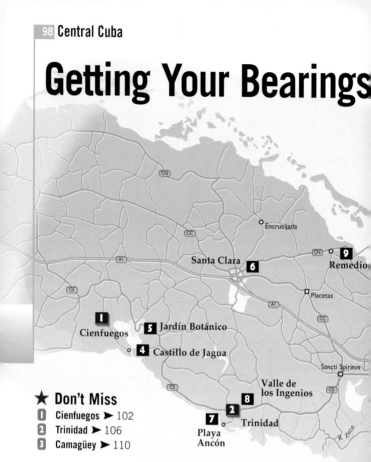

★ **Don't Miss**

1 Cienfuegos ➤ 102
2 Trinidad ➤ 106
3 Camagüey ➤ 110

At Your Leisure

4 Castillo de Nuestra Señora de
los Ángeles de Jagua ➤ 114
5 Jardín Botánico ➤ 114
6 Santa Clara ➤ 114
7 Playa Ancón ➤ 115
8 Valle de los Ingenios ➤ 115
9 Remedios ➤ 116
10 Morón and Cayo Coco ➤ 117

To many visitors, Central Cuba may seem a necessary (if convenient) corridor between Havana and the culturally more exciting east of the country. Nevertheless, it does have much to offer, including the sophisticated and cultured cities of Cienfuegos and Camagüey, as well as the twin architectural jewels of Remedios and Trinidad. The central towns of Santa Clara, Sancti Spiritus and Ciego de Ávila are pleasant, but have little to offer in the way of classical architecture and other attractions.

The causeway to Cayo Coco
Previous page: Oxcart and royal pines, Jardín Botánico

Away from the central spine – the *Carretera Central* (Central Highway) and the main railway line linking Havana with Santiago de Cuba, as well as the uncompleted *autopista* which peters out just north of Jatibonico – it's another matter altogether. The northern coast of Central Cuba is distinguished by the Jardines del Rey (Gardens of the King) – a long, lush range of tropical keys just offshore, many now easily accessible by massive causeways, offering some of the best beach resorts on the island. The same is true of the southern coast, where the more distant Jardines de la Reina (Gardens of the Queen) are less accessible but arguably more exclusive.

Then there's the Sierra del Escambray, a magnificent and almost untouristed range of saw-toothed mountains between Cienfuegos and Trinidad, offering one of the best drives on the island.

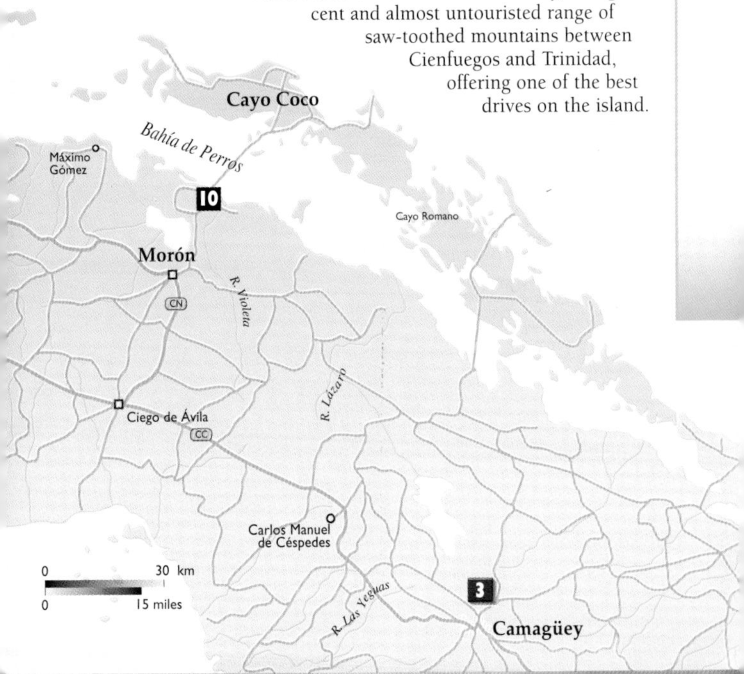

Cayo Coco

Bahía de Perros

Máximo Gómez

10

Morón
(CN)

R. Violeta

Cayo Romano

R. Lázaro

Ciego de Ávila
(CC)

Carlos Manuel de Céspedes

R. Las Yeguas

3

Camagüey

0 ___ 30 km
0 ___ 15 miles

Central Cuba in Three Days

Day One

Morning
Rise early and explore **1** **Cienfuegos'** (➤ 102) central Parque José Martí area before heading to the southern part of town to visit the extraordinary Palacio de Valle. Buy a packed lunch and head off to the nearby **5** **Jardín Botánico** (➤ 114).

Afternoon
Drive through the beautiful **Sierra del Escambray** (➤ 159) perhaps stopping for a picnic meal at El Salto de Hanabanilla (➤ 160).

Evening/night
Arrive in **2** **Trinidad** (➤ 106) in time for what is usually a golden sunset. Enjoy a drink and a meal in one of the bars or restaurants around Parque Céspedes.

Day Two

Morning
Set out early to visit the **8** **Valle de los Ingenios** (➤ 115) and Manaca Iznaga, also in the valley, just half an hour east of Trinidad or head off to nearby **7** **Playa Ancón** (➤ 115) for a swim.

Afternoon
Drive northeast pausing to enjoy lunch in Sancti Spiritus at the Hotel Plaza on

Parque Serafín Sánchez. You now have the choice of heading north to the medieval town of **⑨ Remedios** (► 116) or turning east along the *Carretera Central* to the historic city of **⑧ Camagüey** (► 110).

Evening/night
If you chose Remedios, enjoy dinner at the excellent Hotel Mascotte (► 119). If Camagüey, stay in the equally fine Hotel Colón (► 118).

Day Three

Morning
From Remedios, drive north via the fishing port of Caibarién to take the causeway to the beach resort of Cayo Santa María (above). If in Camagüey, explore the old city around Plaza de los Trabajadores.

Afternoon
At Cayo Santo Maria, sunbathe, swim and relax. From Camagüey drive north through **⑩ Morón** to **Cayo Coco** (► 117) for some idyllic relaxation by the sea.

Evening/night
Enjoy a well-earned rest and a good meal at the Melia Cayo Coco resort, or the Villa Las Brujas on Cayo Santa María.

Cienfuegos

With almost 150,000 inhabitants, Cienfuegos is a large city by Cuban standards. It's also of great strategic importance, located on the east side of the beautiful Bahía de Cienfuegos, possibly Cuba's finest natural harbour. The strategic significance of the bay was recognised long before the city was built. Because the area was unsettled but the bay sheltered and secure it developed into a haven for pirates, obliging the Spanish authorities to build a fortress, the Castillo de Jagua (➤ 114), at the western mouth of the bay in the early 18th century to deny them access.

It wasn't until around 1820 that serious settlement began in Cienfuegos itself. The first colonists came from Bordeaux in France, setting an example that was soon followed by other French colonialists in the New World. Many French refugees from the 1791 revolution in Haiti, when the black slave leader Toussaint Louverture overthrew French rule, fled to Cienfuegos as a place of refuge and resettlement. Then came French refugees from Louisiana after Napoleon sold the territory to the United States in 1803, further reinforcing the French connection. As a consequence many Cubans claim that the people of Cienfuegos have a higher percentage of blonde hair and blue eyes than elsewhere in the island. There is, however, a palpably French feel to some of the city's parks, tree-lined boulevards and buildings.

The elaborate Moorish-style Palacio de Valle

The Historic Centre

Cienfuegos is built on a grid pattern which makes it easy to find your way about. The main north-south boulevard is **Paseo del Prado**, running from the city's southernmost tip at Punta Gorda through

the town centre to the main road to Havana in the north. The oldest and most interesting part of town lies astride and a little to the west of Paseo del Prado, and is centred on **Parque José Martí**, another shrine to the national hero whose white marble statue dominates the park.

The red dome of Palacio Ferrer rises above Parque José Martí

Parque José Martí, one of the finest municipal parks anywhere in the country, is the best place to begin any exploration of Cienfuegos, partly because the square is dominated by so many distinguished buildings, but also because the roads around **Avenue 54** and **Calle 33** to the east of the square are an attractive pedestrian shopping centre.

On the east side of the park stands the neo-classical **Catedral de la Purísima Concepción**, built in 1869 and distinguished by two fine towers and imported French stained-glass windows featuring the 12 apostles. It's worth entering for its Corinthian altar and high, vaulted ceiling which makes it cool during the heat of midday. Outside, facing the shaded square and the statue of Martí, are two white marble lions. To the north of the square is the renowned **Teatro Tomás Terry**, built in 1899 to seat an audience of 950 in an Italian-style auditorium constructed of Cuban cedar. Famous performers who appeared here in the theatre's heyday include Sarah Bernhardt, Enrico Caruso and Anna Pavlova. Although no such luminaries appear there at present, the theatre remains an elegant neo-classical building and one of the architectural gems of Cienfuegos.

Art and Music

Continuing round the square anticlockwise, the next distinguished building is the neo-classical **Colegio San Lorenzo**, right next to **Salon Centro de Arte**, a gallery which offers excellent exhibitions of modern Cuban art. West of the square is the **Casa de la Cultura Benjamin Duarte**, in the **Palacio Ferrer** – a building in sad need of repair and a new coat of paint but with a tower which may be ascended for fine views

Children playing ball in the colonnaded arcades off Parque José Martí

over the town and bay. Occasional performances of live music are given here in the evenings.

A further row of distinguished buildings on the south side of the square complete Cienfuegos' Parque José Martí. These include the **Museo Provincial**, displaying a wide selection of artefacts dating from pre-Columbian times to the bourgeois trappings of life in late colonial Cienfuegos, and the **Galeria Maroya** art gallery. Finally, the **Ayuntamiento de Cienfuegos**, or Provincial Government of Cienfuegos - closed to the public but with a fine red dome – dominates the southeastern corner.

Etching in the Salon Centro de Arte

Away from central Cienfuegos, the city's most extraordinary site is the Moorish-style **Palacio de Valle**, at the southern end of Paseo del Prado in the formerly up-market district of Punta Gorda. This unusual building – which would seem more in place in Seville or Tangiers than in Cienfuegos – was commissioned in 1913 by a local businessman, Aciclio de Valle y Blanco, who employed skilled craftsmen from Morocco to construct a Moorish palace in authentic style. Unlike the central *kiosko* in Manzanillo (► 140) the Arabic text recurring in and around the murals of the Palacio de Valle is authentic and well-executed. Today the Palacio functions as a chic restaurant and small museum. A speciality of the palace

is the piano and cabaret show put on by Carmen, a friendly
if flamboyant transvestite who wears elaborate "Arabian"
style dress.

Away from the Centre

One further historical monument worthy of a visit is the
Cementerio La Reina (Queen's Cemetery), way out in the
west of town on a small peninsula projecting into
Cienfuegos Bay. Established in 1837, this extravagant but
rundown cemetery is notable for the numerous graves of
Spanish soldiers who died during the wars of Cuban independence.

For a more contemporary sobering experience and
memento mori, raise your eyes and look west. In the
distance, across the beautiful bay, a huge concrete dome can
be seen on the horizon. This is the unfinished **Jaragua
Nuclear Power Plant**, begun in cooperation with the
Soviet authorities in 1982 with a view to producing around
10 per cent of Cuba's electrical generating capacity. Work
stalled in 1990 with the collapse of the Soviet
Union and is now at a
standstill. Not all
Cienfuegans seem
dismayed, however –
"that might have been
Cuba's Chernobyl" is a
common (if discreet) view
held by many locals.

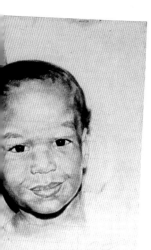

TAKING A BREAK

Try the **Palacio de Valle**
(► 121) or one of the
coffee shops to the east of
Parque José Martí.

➕ 182 B4
Teatro Tomás Terry
✉ Avenida 56 and Calle 27
🕐 Daily 9–6
💰 Inexpensive

Museo Provincial
✉ Avenida 54 and Calle 27
🕐 Tue–Sat 9–4:30
💰 Inexpensive

CIENFUEGOS: INSIDE INFO

Top tip Check out the art gallery next to Colegio San Lorenzo – it features the
work of some of the **best contemporary artists** in Cienfuegos.

Hidden gem Every other year in September the **Benny Moré International
Festival of Popular Music** takes place in various venues around town.

② Trinidad

The small settlement of Trinidad, nestled in the lee of the Sierra del Escambray, ranks as the most authentically medieval town in Cuba. This was recognised even before the Cuban Revolution, during the time of the dictator Batista, as during the mid-1950s Trinidad was officially declared a "National Monument" and any unauthorised new construction was forbidden. This sensible policy was reinforced in 1988 when both Trinidad and the neighbouring Valle de los Ingenios (► 115) were declared World Heritage Sites by UNESCO.

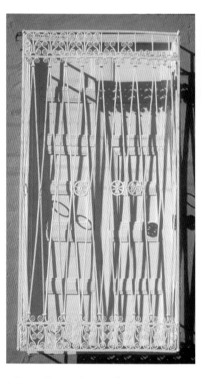

Ornate window grille in Old Trinidad

Trinidad – really little more than a large village with a population of around 30,000 – was founded by Diego Velázquez in 1514 as Cuba's third European colonial settlement. Initially it prospered as a gold-mining centre, and also as a base of operations for the conquistador Hernán Cortés during his 1518 invasion and conquest of Mexico. Subsequently, Havana suceeded Trinidad as the main base for Spanish operations against the Central American mainland, but by this time the fertile soil around Trinidad was already replacing locally mined and Mexican gold with sugar cane.

Wealth Based On Sugar

During the 18th century Trinidad and the neighbouring Valle de Los Ingenios entered their boom period. Fortunes were made, fine buildings, both religious and mundane, were constructed, and the town acquired an elegant dignity which still survives, despite years of isolation and poverty after the local sugar industry was eclipsed by provinces to the north. Today as tourism rapidly becomes Cuba's main source of over-

seas income, Trinidad looks set to embark on its third period
of economic prosperity. If so, this delightful little town may
long survive and flourish.

Trinidad is tucked into the surrounding hills to its north
and east. It also rises perceptibly upwards away from the sea
towards the old town centre. This makes walking difficult –
the more so since the entire old town is cobbled in a very
rough fashion, with uneven blocks of stone sloping inwards
to a central gutter. Local legend has it that the first mayor had
one leg shorter than the other and designed the town in this
fashion to facilitate his getting around, but in fact it used to
be pretty standard middle ages town drainage.

The Commercial Centre

Most visitors entering Trinidad will head for the south-central
Parque Céspedes where the main hotels and restaurants are
located. It's best to stay here and walk uphill and inland to the
Plaza Mayor, which is the historic heart of old Trinidad.
Simple, pastel-coloured houses with red shingle-tiled roofs
and elaborate window grilles line every street, often with
older residents sitting on the porch in rocking chairs just
watching time pass.

It takes about 20 minutes to reach Plaza Mayor from
Parque Céspedes. Plaza Mayor is a delightful shaded square
surrounded by colonial buildings. It's especially glorious at
sunset on a clear day, when the town's southwest orientation
causes the last, auburn-gold rays of the sun to illuminate the
upper town in an almost faerie-like glow.

A Town of Churches

The square is dominated to the north (uphill) by the **Iglesia
Parroquial de la Santísima Trinidad**. The baroque front is
magnificent, and inside is a venerated statue, Christ of the
True Cross, in the centre of an altar to the left. Trinidad is a
staunchly Catholic town, and if you can, visit during services

**Trinidad street
scene at sunset**

or at Mass (8pm weekdays, 4pm Saturday, 5pm Sunday). The music features guitars and maracas as well as an organ, and the Cuban element is very apparent.

Further up the hill, about 500m (545 yards) behind the Iglesia Parroquial, is the decrepit but lovely **Ermita de Nuestra Señora de la Candelaria de la Popa**. Long scheduled for restoration, the main entrance remains bricked up for safety reasons, but the triple spire at the front of this former Spanish military hospital and church has become something of a symbol of Trinidad. From here, on a clear day, you can see right across town to the blue Caribbean.

Other sights around the Plaza Mayor include the **Museo Romántico**, to the northwest of the Iglesia Parroquial. Originally built as the Palacio Brunet in 1740, the artefacts on display represent the lifestyles of affluent Trinidadians in the 19th century, when sugar was still king. On the southeast side of the square the mid-18th-century **Museo de Arquitectura** displays similar artefacts as well as providing examples of different styles of local architecture over the last two centuries. Finally, on the west side of the square, the **Museo de Arqueología Guamuhaya** features a mix of natural history and pre-Columbian Indian artefacts.

Bell tower of the former Convent of San Francisco de Asís

Santería Traditions

Unusually for this part of Cuba there's a Santería temple, the **Casa Templo de Santería Yemayá** just a few metres to the west of Plaza Mayor at Villena 59. Santería is more closely associated with the Afro-Caribbean tradition, while Trinidad is very old-world Spanish. Here you can consult Santería priests, have your fortune told and seek blessings from various *orishas* (gods). A little further to the north, and dominating the whole square, stands the tall spire of the former convent of San Francisco de Asís, now the **Museo Nacional de la Lucha Contra Bandidos**, featuring displays of the military campaign against anti-Castro guerrillas in the nearby Sierra del Escambray during the 1970s. There are fine views across both the town and the mountains from the top of the bell tower, especially in the mornings.

TAKING A BREAK

It's great to relax with a local beer and a jar of olives in the Plaza Mayor towards sunset as the square is taken over by local children scooting about and playing on bicycles. For dinner head back to the Parque Céspedes area and try **La Ronda** (➤ 121) and its creole cuisine.

🔢 182 C3
Museo Romántico
✉ Calle Fernando Hernández
Echerri 52
🕐 Tue–Sun 9–5
✋ Inexpensive

Museo de Arquitectura
✉ Plaza Mayor
🕐 Sat–Thu 8–5
✋ Inexpensive

Museo de Arqueología Guamuhaya
✉ Calle Simón Bolívar 457
🕐 Sun–Fri 9–5
✋ Inexpensive

Museo Nacional de la Lucha Contra Bandidos
✉ Calle Echerri 59
🕐 Tue–Sat 9–noon, 2–6, Sun 9–1
✋ Inexpensive

TRINIDAD: INSIDE INFO

Top tip Trinidad is unusual in Cuba both for the quality and quantity of the **art-work and local souvenirs** on sale. There are **galleries** scattered around the cobbled streets near Plaza Mayor, and private houses sometimes display oil or water paintings as well as charcoal line drawings of Trinidad on their front porches.

3 Camagüey

Camagüey is Cuba's third largest, and least easily navigable city. With a population in excess of 300,000 it's not a small place, yet the streets are often unbelievably narrow and tortuous. Forget the easy grid system employed in most Cuban cities, here it simply doesn't exist. Even so, Camagüey has a great deal to offer the visitor.

Stained-glass window in the Catedral de Nuestra Señora de la Candelaria

But why exactly are the streets so narrow and so twisting? The locals have an easy explanation. Although, unlike Cuba's other major cities, Camagüey is centred inland and not on the coast, it was still considered liable to pirate raids by its founders in 1528. It was thought that an irregular and unpredictable street plan would confuse and disorientate any such invaders – but it just didn't work. The English privateer Sir Henry Morgan comprehensively sacked the town in 1668, and the French pirate François Granmont duplicated this exploit in 1679. The buccaneers are long since gone, but the road system remains, and unfortunately it now does an excellent job of confusing and disorientating the visitor. Be prepared to park (if you can find a space) and walk – the distances are not great, and it is worth it.

Park and Walk

Camagüey is situated on the *Carretera Central* and until a ring road was recently built there was the most terrible bottleneck. Now it's easy to circumnavigate the town to the north,

but watch out for hustlers who will try and force you the way they want you to go by driving bicycles or motorcycles at an angle in front of your vehicle. Be prepared, ignore them, and if they follow you pay no attention – head for the city's main north-south road, Calle República, which is so narrow that two vehicles can barely pass at the same time. The crossroads where República meets Avenida Agramonte are the nearest thing Camagüey has to a town centre. Turn west here along Agramonte to find a supervised car park (US$1) at the **Plaza de los Trabajadores**.

A quiet moment on Plaza San Juan de Dios

Christ figure, Iglesia de Nuestra Señora de la Merced

The Plaza de los Trabajadores is dominated on its east side by the **Iglesia de Nuestra Señora de la Merced**, completed in 1776. The outside, constructed of worn red brick, is massive rather than elegant. The interior is splendid, however, with some fine examples of baroque frescoes and an unusual vaulted ceiling. There is a convent in the neighbouring cloister, so make allowance for the nuns when taking photographs or just sight-seeing. On the west side of the plaza stands the neo-classical **Teatro Guerrero**, while immediately to the south the main post office is dominated by a steel silhouette of the unmistakable features of Che Guevara, reminiscent (on a smaller scale) of that in Havana's Plaza de la Revolución. Next to the post office is the **Museo Casa Natal de Ignacio Agramonte**, a small but attractive museum where Ignacio Agramonte, Camagüey's most famous warrior in the fight for independence from Spain, was born in 1841. Agramonte led a major attack against the Spanish forces occupying Camagüey in 1869, but was killed four years later in another action against the Spanish colonialists. The house has been beautifully restored and is well worth a visit.

Southwest of the plaza, about 150m (163 yards) along Calle Cisneros, a small side road leads left (west) for a few metres to the **Casa Natal de Nicolás Guillén** – an attractive modernistic brass plaque marks the place where this famous poet was born in 1902. Guillén founded a school of Afro-Caribbean poetry and was the nation's poet laureate until his death in 1989.

Hot dog seller, Camagüey

South of the Centre

Further south, Calle Cisneros leads directly to **Parque Ignacio Agramonte**, a fine civic square distinguished by a statue of Agramonte, Camagüey's local hero, on horseback. The park is dominated by the **Catedral de Nuestra Señora de la Candelaria** on the south side. Dating from 1530, the church was essentially rebuilt in the 19th century and has been restored. There are two fine stained-glass windows, as well as an unusual statue of a black priest – San Benito di Palermo – inside. Immediately to the west of the church is Camagüey's rather battered **Casa de la Trova** where live music can be heard throughout the week.

Further south again, about 200m (218 yards) along Paco Recio, the narrow road opens out into **Plaza San Juan de Dios**. This is Camagüey's most distinguished and atmospheric square, lined on the north by some of the city's finest restaurants – look for the *tinajones*, or huge earthenware water-storage jars which have become a symbol of Camagüey in the garden of the Campana de Toledo restaurant. The whole of the western side of the square – where young children in school uniform are often to be seen exercising – is dominated by the **Hospital de San Juan de Dios**, a former hospital which now functions as the Centro Provincial de Patrimonio, the office in charge of restoring historic Camagüey. This fine building, with a rather restrained exterior, is notable for its front cloister dating from the early 18th century.

Besides the excellent restaurants on Plaza San Juan de Dios,

Right: Children at a fun-fair, Camagüey

the **Hotel Colón** (► 118) is worth a mention. North of the Plaza de los Trabajadores on Calle República, this fine old colonial hotel has been beautifully restored and features a stained-glass image of Christopher Columbus above the doorway leading from the main hallway to the open-air Patio Bar. The bar and restaurant is surrounded by twisting, pastel-painted pillars supporting the first floor balcony.

TAKING A BREAK
Stop for a break at **La Campana de Toledo** (► 120).

🚩 183 F2

Museo Casa Natal de Ignacio Agramonte
✉ Avenida Ignacio Agramante 459
🕐 Tue–Sat 10–5, Sun 8––noon
🎟 Inexpensive

Casa Natal de Nicolás Guillén
✉ Calle Hermano Agüero
🕐 Mon–Fri 8–4:30
🎟 Inexpensive

Hospital de San Juan de Dios
✉ Plaza San Juan de Dios
🕐 Mon–Sat 8–5
🎟 Inexpensive

CAMAGÜEY: INSIDE INFO

Top tip During April and May Camagüey holds the **Festival de Arte Danzario**, an international festival of dance.

Hidden gem A quiet place to relax in the shade away from the main tourist attractions is **Casino Campestre**, a large area ideal for a few moments of reflection, relaxation and watching the locals. It's about 400m (436 yards) due east of Plaza San Juan de Dios, and is served by regular horse carts.

At Your Leisure

❹ Castillo de Nuestra Señora de los Ángeles de Jagua

The earliest building in Cienfuegos – built long before the town of Cienfuegos was founded – this venerable Spanish colonial castle dates from 1745. The fort's original purpose was to deny buccaneers access to the sheltered but isolated Bahía de Cienfuegos and in its time it was one of the strongest Spanish military bastions on the island. It's situated on the western side of the narrow entrance to Cienfuegos Bay, and can be reached by ferry. Alternatively take a 20-minute drive from central Cienfuegos to La Milpa and then from here a 10-minute boat ride by regular ferry across the narrows. There's a government restaurant specialising in seafood within the castle, but the main attraction is the external view of the Castillo de Jagua itself and the small but picturesque fishing village it dominates.

✚ 182 B3 ✉ 9km (5.6 miles) south of Cienfuegos ⏰ Daily 8–4 ▒ Inexpensive ⛴ Ferry from Calle 25 and Avenida 46, Cienfuegos

❺ Jardín Botánico

These charming but somewhat neglected gardens can be visited as an excursion from Cienfuegos, or as part of a drive through the nearby Sierra del Escambray (➤ 159) either to or from Trinidad (➤ 106). Situated near the Pepito Tey sugar factory, 18km (11 miles) east of Cienfuegos, the gardens were founded by Edward F. Atkins, a US sugar baron who made millions on his estates in Cuba at the beginning of the 20th century. Atkins' original intention was to develop and improve different varieties of sugar cane, but this soon became a passion for collecting rare and unusual botanical specimens from Cuba,

the Caribbean and further afield.

The gardens – more properly known as Jardín Botánico Soledad – were taken over by Harvard University in 1920 and administered by it until the 1960s. They are difficult to reach except by taxi or private car. Though rather run-down, they still shelter more than 2,000 species of plants, including many spectacular bamboos and more than 200 varieties of palms.

✚ 182 B4 ✉ 16km (10 miles) east of Cienfuegos ⏰ Daily 8–4 ▒ Moderate

❻ Santa Clara

Santa Clara, the capital of Villa Clara Province, is a large city by Cuban standards – it has more than 200,000 inhabitants – but with relatively little to offer. The main square, Parque

At the Jardín Botánico

Vidal, is reached by a grid of narrow streets and has been thankfully closed to traffic. The park is distinguished by a number of fine though dilapidated buildings, notably the Teatro La Caridad (1885) and the neo-classical Palacio Provincial (1910). Next to the theatre the **Museo de Artes Decorativas** houses a good collection of colonial antiques and paintings.

The main attraction in Santa Clara is the **Monumento Ernesto Che Guevara**, a huge shrine to the revolutionary hero, with his arm in a sling and carrying a rifle. It was erected in 1987 to mark the 20th anniversary of Guevara's execution in Bolivia, and in 1997 his disinterred remains were reburied here amid much pomp and ceremony. There's a museum of Guevara memorabilia behind the monument, and revolutionary guards stand about to make sure proper respect is shown – no sitting on the monument steps, for example. This shrine to Che and the Cuban Revolution is on Avenida de los Desfiles in the west of the city.

🚺 182 C4

The watchtower at Manaca Iznaga

Museo de Artes Decorativas
✉ Parque Vidal 🕐 Mon–Fri 9–5, Sat 1–9:30 💶 Inexpensive

Monumento Ernesto Che Guevara and Museum
✉ Plaza de la Revolución, Avenida de los Desfiles 🕐 Tue–Sat 8–9, Sun 8–6 💶 Free

🔟 Playa Ancón

This beach resort, on the Caribbean coast close to Trinidad (➤ 106) has some fine powder-white beaches and is an excellent venue for diving and snorkelling, with good coral reefs not far offshore. Unfortunately it's a long way from anywhere (except Trinidad) and can't really match up to the larger and much better

equipped beach resorts of the north coast such as Varadero (➤ 88) and Cayo Coco (➤ 117). However, it's a good place for a couple of days sun, sea and sand relaxation on a visit to Trinidad, but not large enough to warrant a one or two week holiday. Birdwatchers will find numerous species of water birds, including heron and crane, which inhabit the quiet reaches of **Ensenada de Casilda**, a shallow bay almost cut off from the Caribbean by the Peninsula de Ancón.

🚺 182 C3 ✉ 15km (9.3 miles) south of Trinidad

Ensenada de Casilda
✉ 1km (0.6 mile) northeast of Playa Ancón

🔟 Valle de los Ingenios

Once one of the richest sugar regions in Cuba, the Valle de los Ingenios (Valley of the Sugar Mills) is today a remarkably picturesque region, evocative of the Trinidad area's rich,

Parroquial de San Juan Bautista, Remedios

built, but it may have been to keep a watchful eye on the slaves labouring in the cane fields all around. It's a tiring but exhilarating climb.

🚹 182 C3

Manaca Iznaga
✉ 12km (7.4 miles) east of Trinidad
🕐 Daily 8–5 💰 Inexpensive

❾ Remedios

Although much smaller than Trinidad, Remedios is the second jewel in the crown of Cuba's rustic medieval heritage. Founded in 1524, it was eclipsed by Santa Clara in the late 17th century and has changed relatively little since. The main square, Plaza Martí, is dominated by two churches – the 18th-century Iglesia de Nuestra Señora del Buen Viaje with a fine bell tower, and the more important **Parroquial de San Juan Bautista**, dating from 1545.

The latter is certainly one of the most beautiful churches in Cuba, particularly notable for its elaborately carved and gilded altar, as well as the only statue of a pregnant Madonna of the Immaculate Conception in Cuba, or as the locals claim, in the world.

At the centre of Plaza Martí is the Kiosko Pando, a bandstand dating from 1909, where live "big band" music is played weekly on Thursday nights. Remedios is also famous for the Festival of Parrandas which takes place annually on 24 and 25 December, during which the locals dance and sing while Remedios' main districts compete for the honour of the best *carroza* or float. It's a delightful little town, boasting Hotel

sugar-based past. The valley, east of Trinidad, is dotted with the crumbling ruins of many small sugar mills and estates. Just before reaching the valley a narrow turn to the left, roughly 6km (3.7 miles) from Trinidad, leads to the Mirador de La Loma del Puerto, an attractive viewpoint with fine views across the valley to the north and east.

The main monument in the valley is at **Manaca Iznaga**, a once-affluent sugar estate founded in the late 18th century. Dominated by a 45m (148ft)-high watchtower standing next to the hacienda, the estate is today a major attraction, served by a restored steam train which takes visitors from Trinidad to enjoy lunch at the excellent restaurant Manaca Iznaga in the restored hacienda. Outside you can view the old sugar mill machinery and bargain for good-quality, locally made lace. Nobody seems to know why the tower was

Mascotte, a beautifully restored colonial hotel, and makes a perfect stopover en route to nearby Cayo Santa María.

➕ 182 C4

Parroquial de San Juan Bautista
✉ Plaza Martí 🕐 Sun–Fri 9–5, Sat 9–12

⑩ Morón and Cayo Coco

The medium-sized town of Morón, about 40km (25 miles) north of Ciego de Ávila on the *Carretera Central*, serves as a gateway to the

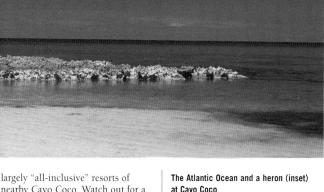

largely "all-inclusive" resorts of nearby Cayo Coco. Watch out for a large iron cockerel – the symbol of Morón – near the town centre, as well as a rather distinguished late 19th-century railway station. Then push on across the 27km (16.7 miles) causeway that carries traffic over the shallow Bahía de Perros to Cayo Coco, one of Cuba's fastest-developing beach destinations. This resort area in the Jardines del Rey Archipiélago offers first-class accommodation, plenty of good buffet food,

The Atlantic Ocean and a heron (inset) at Cayo Coco

and fine beaches. There are also smaller causeways leading to isolated Cayo Guillermo in the west and Cayo Romano to the east. There's good deep-sea fishing, and an abundance of wildlife, including flocks of double-crested cormorants in the mangrove swamps that surround the southern parts of the islands and along the causeways.

➕ 183 E4

Where to... Stay

Prices

Expect to pay per double room per night

$ under US$50 $$ US$50–150 $$$ over US$150

CAMAGÜEY

Colón $$

Camagüey's finest hotel, and really a pleasure to stay in. The main lobby has a wonderful old bar where the friendly English-speaking bartender serves an elaborate variety of cocktails. As you enter the hotel from the lobby, note the stained-glass visage of Christopher Columbus (Cristóbal Colón in Spanish, hence the hotel's name) over the door. This is followed by a long and stately corridor draped with national flags including that of the United States, Britain and France, but not North Korea or China. The hotel has been reno-vated and updated. There's just one serious drawback – there are no car parking facilities, and the road outside is so narrow that you have no alternative but to drive to the supervised car park in the Plaza de los Trabajadores and walk back – about 10 minutes – to the hotel.

🔢 183 F2 ⊠ Avenida República 472
☎ (322) 83380

Gran Hotel $

This is another fine old hotel that has undergone extensive restoration. Five storeys high, overlooking the heart of the old city, there is a period charm to the place which lends appeal to the somewhat rickety elevator. Rooms are clean, service good and friendly, and best of all there's a rather elegant restaurant offering wonderful views and filling *criollo* cuisine on the top floor. There's a period-style piano bar just off the lobby, but as with other establishments in central Camagüey, parking can be a problem.

🔢 183 F2 ⊠ Calle Maceo 67, between Agramonte and Gómez
☎ (322) 92093

CAYO COCO

Meliá Cayo Coco $$$

A very large, well-appointed establishment (under Spanish management) which definitely aims at the all-in package tour market, but will generally take independent travellers. As you would expect, the hotel has just about everything from numerous bars, restaurants, a large swimming pool and email facilities to shops and a taxi service. The decor is classically Iberian and the gardens and pools are beauti-fully landscaped. Meals tend to be buffet rather than à la carte, and the quality is both fresh and good. A little bit of the Costa Brava set down, unexpectedly, in central Cuba, this is probably the shape of things to come along the nation's many offshore keys.

🔢 183 E4 ⊠ Playa los Coloradas
☎ (33) 301180; fax: (33) 301195

CAYO SANTA MARÍA

Villa Las Brujas $$

An idyllic setting overlooking the Atlantic Ocean. The beautiful villas are connected by walkways just above the mangroves. There's a good restaurant serving *criollo*, Spanish and international food, as well as a poolside bar for cocktails at sundown. The hotel management can arrange for various watersports, but most people will be content to lay back in the comfortable recliners, iced drink in hand.

🔢 183 D4 ⊠ Cayo Las Brujas
☎ (42) 204199; fax: (42) 207599

CIENFUEGOS

Jagua $$

Originally built in the 1950s by Cuban dictator Fulgencio Batista's brother, this hotel has been fully restored and is now run as a joint Cuban-French venture overseen by the French hotel giant Accor. It comes highly recommended, but it isn't cheap. Amenities include a swimming pool, tennis courts, money exchange facilities, car rentals, a post office and a taxi stand. There's a nightly cabaret by the swimming pool, starting at 9:30, for US$8 (including first drink). The restaurant is good, with Spanish, French and Italian dishes providing a welcome alternative to the nourishing but often bland cocina criolla. Accor has made sure the wine list is longer than usual in Cienfuegos, with vintages from Europe and the New World.

➕ 182 B4 ⌧ 1, Calle 37, Punta Gorda ☎ (432) 513021/26; fax: (432) 667454

Rancho Luna $$

Located 18km (11 miles) south of town by the shores of the Caribbean Sea, this large resort has its own private beach and restaurants – which is just as well, as there's nowhere else to eat nearby. Popular with more affluent Cubans (including residents of Florida on holiday) as well as nouveau riche locals, the main activities include swimming, scuba diving and snorkelling. There's a horse-and-buggy service for riding along the shoreline, while facilities include various shops, a pharmacy and car rental services. The main attractions are the warm waters of the Caribbean and the plentiful seafood.

➕ 182 B4 ⌧ Carretera de Rancho Luna, Playa Rancho Luna ☎ (432) 514812; fax: (432) 548131

MORÓN

Morón $$

There's little aesthetically pleasing about this hotel, which lacks character and offers a pretty disinterested service, but it's still easily the best place to stay in Morón, with comfortable if standard rooms. The restaurant serves reasonable criollo dishes, a filling but rather bland buffet breakfast (not included in the overall price, it will set you back US$5 a head) and there is a selection of shops and services.

➕ 183 E4 ⌧ Avenida de Tarafa ☎ (335) 3901

REMEDIOS

Mascotte $$

This beautifully restored colonial period hotel with charming staff and a good restaurant overlooks Remedios' historic Parque Martí. The rooms are full of character, with high, sloping ceilings, restored 19th-century bathrooms – including marble wash basins in the main bedrooms – and shuttered windows looking onto the park or the inner courtyard. The only problem is parking, which is not permitted at night in the vicinity of Parque Martí – but for US$2 a hotel employee will take your vehicle to a nearby and secure parking place and return it, at a time of your choosing, in the morning. All-in-all this is one of the nicest places to stay in Cuba. An unexpected gem.

➕ 182 C4 ⌧ Parque Martí and Máximo Gómez ☎ (422) 395144

SANTA CLARA

Los Caneyes $$

Just a short distance west of town on the main ring road, this is a strange but excellent place to stay. Accommodation is in "American Indian" style, comprising thatched, circular buildings (but with hot water and cable TV). There's a swimming pool, car rental service, guarded parking lot and even a small post office. The restaurant, which serves buffet criollo fare, is extensive and good. The carefully tended gardens feature Indian-style sculptures and stone faces set in

Where to...
Eat and Drink

Prices

Expect to pay per person for a two-course meal, excluding drinks and service
$ under US$10 $$ US$10–25 $$$ over US$25

CAMAGÜEY

La Campana de Toledo $$

Perhaps Camagüey's best restaurant, on the north side of Plaza San Juan de Dios, the city's most historic square. The food is definitively *criollo*, but it's well-cooked and tastefully served in an attractive garden setting, complete with traditional giant *tinajones* water jars, the symbol of Camagüey. There's a selection of cold beers on offer, as well as some local Cuban wines. Friendly staff, the quiet, rustic setting and the attractions of the nearby plaza make this an excellent place to break for lunch or to have dinner.

🔢 **183 F2** ⊠ **Plaza San Juan de Dios** ☎ **(322) 95888** 🕐 **Daily 10 am–10 pm**

Hotel Colón $$

The restaurant is located in the charmingly restored inner courtyard, distinguished by elaborate, twisting, pastel-painted columns, with vines growing overhead. The food – *criollo* and international cuisine, with a pretty good wine list – is both tasty and reasonably priced. Although Camagüey is some way inland, the grilled fish is fresh

🔢 **183 F2** ⊠ **Plaza San Juan de Dios** ☎ **(322) 95888** 🕐 **Daily 10 am–10 pm**

---

some tree trunks. Security is noticeable as members of the Cuban communist élite often stay here together with their families...

🔢 **182 C4** ⊠ **Avenida de los Eucaliptos and Circunvalación de Santa Clara** ☎ **(422) 28140**

TRINIDAD

Las Cuevas $$

Just northeast of the town centre, beyond the ruined Iglesia de Santa Ana, this is a large, government-run establishment with well over a hundred rooms in three blocks, plus a swimming pool. It attracts a mixed crowd of foreign visitors and better-off Cubans, but has less atmosphere (and is less centrally located) than Hotel La Ronda. Parking is a lot easier, however, and the standard both of food and accommodation is generally good. The main local attraction Cueva La Maravillosa (from which the hotel gets its name) is accessible via a nearby stairway. There are

exceptional views across Trinidad to the Caribbean.

🔢 **182 C3** ⊠ **1km (0.6 miles) northeast of town at Finca Santa Ana** ☎ **(419) 49139; fax: (419) 6161**

La Ronda $

This restored colonial building near Parque Céspedes is both charming and well-run. There's a good restaurant with tasty and nourishing *criollo* fare, as well as a central courtyard with a bar serving a selection of snacks, cocktails and iced beer. At night there's sometimes live music, especially at weekends, which is cheerful but can be a bit noisy. There's also a parking problem, with room for no more than three or four cars in the narrow street outside the hotel. If so, ask the hotel staff to take your car to a secure park. The rooms are decorated with tastefully executed line drawings of traditional Trinidad architecture.

🔢 **182 C3** ⊠ **Calle José Martí 239** ☎ **(419) 2248**

and tender and comes highly recommended. There's a rather genteel atmosphere about the place, and the service is friendly and efficient. On the other side of the courtyard, a well-stocked bar serves an elaborate menu of cocktails.

�# 183 F2 ☒ Avenida República 472 ☎ (322) 83380 ⓒ Daily 11:30–2:30, 6–10:30

Vicaria Principeña (Nan King) $$

This is another Sino-Cuban establishment, with reasonable oriental-style "Chinese" dishes including sweet-and-sour pork, chop suey, fried noodle dishes (made with what is often spaghetti). spring rolls – as well as the usual *comida criollo* standbys. Lobster, easily the most expensive dish on the menu, is often served grilled or boiled in its own juices *criollo*-fashion and not Chinese-style.

�# 183 F2 ☒ Avenida República 220 ☎ (322) 95455 ⓒ Daily 11–10:30

CIENFUEGOS

Finca La Isabela $$

"Isabela's Ranch" is a country-style restaurant about 3km east of town on the road to Rancho Luna. It specialises in farm-style rural Cuban cuisine and also offers horse-back riding for the authentic *guajiro* feel. The food is fine, the bean soups and baked fish dishes being especially good, the prices are reasonable, and the setting is certainly attractive.

�# 182 B4 ☒ Carretera de Rancho Luna ☎ (432) 547006 ⓒ Daily 11–2, 6–10

Palacio de Valle $$

Quite the opposite to the deliberately rustic Finca La Isabela, the Palacio de Valle is an elaborate palace in Moorish style located in the heart of the up-market southern Cienfuegos district Punta Gorda. The restaurant specialises in seafood, particularly lobster, and there's an excellent rooftop terrace

bar serving cocktails with good views across beautiful Cienfuegos Bay. There's a live pianist, and in the evenings the staff dress in "oriental" clothing. Unusually for Cuba, there's often a transvestite cabaret show. A very stylish place.

�# 182 B4 ☒ Calle 37 and 2, Punta Gorda ☎ (432) 549651 ⓒ Daily 9:30 am–10:30 pm

REMEDIOS

Restaurante Mascotte $$

There's one good reason for eating at the Restaurante Mascotte in Remedios, there's nowhere else in town that offers a better bed or meal. The food is *comida criollo* – Remedios is a long way from Havana – but it's reasonably priced, elegantly presented and served in an attractive colonial-era dining room by the side of Parque Martí.

�# 182 C4 ☒ Parque Martí and Máximo Gómez ☎ (422) 395144 ⓒ Daily 11:30–2, 6–10:30

TRINIDAD

Plaza el Jigue $

A rather slow, state-run place serving tasty *criollo* fare at reasonable rates. The house speciality is *pollo al Jigue* (baked chicken), but it's also a good place for all the usual Cuban standbys – pizza, *papas fritas*, hamburgers, grilled pork and *Moros y Christianos* (rice and black beans).

�# 182 C3 ☒ Calles Martínez Villena and Piro Guinart ☎ (419) 4315 ⓒ Daily 11:30–2:30, 6–10:30

La Ronda $

La Ronda is in the hotel of the same name, close by Parque Céspedes, in an air-conditioned dining room between the lobby and the central courtyard. The food is distinctively Cuban creole cuisine with some minor concessions to international tastes such as spaghetti, pizza and hamburgers. Friendly staff and a convenient location make it a good option – except on Friday and

Saturday nights when the live music from the nearby courtyard can be deafening.

+ 182 C3 ✉ **Calle Martí 239** ☎ **(419) 2248** 🕓 **Daily 11:30–2:30, 6:30–11**

Trinidad Colonial $

The *criollo* cuisine is served in an elegant 19th-century colonial period mansion, the Casa Bidegaray. Both the building and the upscale décor inside suggest that this should be a little more expensive than Trinidad standbys like the Plaza el Jigue, but in fact prices are pretty much the same. Grilled fish fresh from the Caribbean and served with *arroz blanco* is a popular dish, and the salads are more imaginative than the simple plate of cold green beans or sliced cucumber usually offered. Another house speciality is succulent lobster. Definitely worth a visit.

+ 182 C3 ✉ **Calle Maceo 402 at Calle Colón** ☎ **(419) 2873** 🕓 **Daily 11:30–3, 6–10**

Manaca Iznaga $$

Set in a former sugar hacienda which has been lovingly restored. Outside stands the famous seven-storey tower of Manaca Iznaga, and the valley's old sugar locomotive stops nearby, bringing tourists from Trinidad to sample the fare. This includes cold cuts of ham with cheese, *potaje de frijoles* (bean soup), and a number of specialities such as a tasty pork and sweet pepper stew, *pollo guajiro* (farmers' chicken), pork steak "Escambray style" and a good beefsteak (*bistec de res natural*). Unusually, there are also *dulce criollo* (Creole desserts). The restaurant is painted in pastel shades of blue and yellow, with high wooden ceilings and elaborate candelabra. There's a small bar in a separate room to the left. The atmosphere is congenial, and there is an old sugar press at the back.

+ 182 C3 ✉ **Hacienda Manaca Iznaga** ☎ **7241 6338** 🕓 **Daily 9–5**

Where to...
Shop

Central Cuba has several large towns including Cienfuegos, Santa Clara and Camagüey, as well as the beach resorts of Cayo Coco and Playa Ancón. There's also the important historical destination of Trinidad. All have something to offer the visitor in the way of shopping, while Trinidad has the best quality art markets beyond Havana and Santiago de Cuba.

Souvenirs

The government-run hotel chains maintain the best-stocked general souvenir shops in the Central Region – often not just the best, but the only ones. Cienfuegos is a pleasant place to shop by provincial Cuban standards. Avenida 54 from Parque José Martí to Calle 37, known locally as **El Boulevard**, is a well-maintained pedestrian shopping zone with numerous shops selling souvenirs, as well as cigar and rum outlets. The shops are interspersed with small cafés and restaurants.

Shopping in **Santa Clara** is more restricted, but here another '**Boulevard**', on Independencia between Calles Maceo and Zayas, is a pedestrian shopping mall with a couple of souvenir shops – Santa Clara gets relatively few tourists. **Calle Maceo** is the main shopping street in **Camagüey**, with a number of souvenir shops, bookstalls, mini-marts and small eateries.

Arts and Crafts

In **Cienfuegos** go to **Artex El Topacio** at Avenida 54 No 3510 for music and books. The **Fondo Cubano de Bienes Culturales** on the south side of Parque José Martí has an excellent gallery of local art for sale, as does the **Salon Centro de Arte** on the opposite side.

Where to...
Be Entertained

Santa Clara is less well known for its arts, but the **Fondo Cubano de Bienes Culturales** at Calle Luis Estévez Norte 9 sells local handicrafts, while **La Verbena** at Calle Colon 18 is the best music shop in town.

Camagüey is Cuba's third largest city and this is reflected in the quality of its arts and crafts shops. **Galería ACAA** on **Plaza de los Trabajores** sells local handicrafts and paintings. The best music shop in town is **Tiends El Cartel** at Calle Cisneros 208, just off Parque Agramonte. Also good are **Video Center Imágenes** at Avenida República 282, and **Artex Souvenir** at Avenida República 381.

The real place to go for fine Cuban art, however, is the medieval town of **Trinidad** where many artisans have set up shop. Paintings, etchings, carvings, Santeria religious artefacts and T-shirts are for sale all over town, but especially at the **Arts-and-Crafts Market** on **Calle Jesús Menéndez** by the Casa

de la Trova. There's also the **Bazar Trinidad** at Calle Maceo 451, and the **Fondo Cubano de Bienes Culturales** at Calle Bolívar 48, just off Plaza Mayor.

Imported Goods

All the provincial capitals of Central region – not just **Cienfuegos**, **Santa Clara** and **Camagüey**, but also **Sancti Spiritus** and **Ciego de Avila** – have branches of the hard-currency chain **Tiendas Panamericanas**. These can be invaluable if you're driving yourself, as they are just about the only place to stock up on imported foodstuffs, toiletries and other minor luxuries. Otherwise head to the major hotels in the big cities and especially at isolated all-in resorts such as **Cayo Coco** and **Playa Ancón**. Also worth checking in Cienfuegos known as **El Boulevard** where it's sometimes possible to buy imported film and other "luxury goods".

The Central Cuban cities of Cienfuegos, Santa Clara and Camagüey are comparatively rich, and support flourishing art and cultural scenes aimed primarily at local people. By contrast the beach resorts of Playa Ancón and Cayo Coco target the tourist market and this is reflected in the number of bars and discos. The much smaller towns of Trinidad and Remedios fall into yet another category – tourist destinations with cultural appeal.

The Arts

The most distinguished theatre in Cienfuegos is **Teatro Tomás Terry** on Parque José Martí. Musical performances here feature everything from classical to *salsa*. The

Teatro Guiñol at 5416 Calle 37 presents puppet shows for children on Saturday and Sunday mornings at 10 am.

In Santa Clara the **Casa de la Cultura Juan Marinello** at Parque Vidal 5 gives concerts and occasional art exhibitions, while **Club Mejunje** at Calle Marta Abreu 107 provides traditional music daily except Mondays and children's theatre on Sundays at 10 am.

Camagüey is home to the world-class **Camagüey Ballet** which gives regular performances at the **Teatro Principal**, Calle Padre Valencia 64. Folk musicians play regularly at the **Casa de la Trova Patricio Ballegas** at Calle Cisneros 171.

Trinidad stages performances of the **Trinidad Folk Ensemble** nightly (except Monday) at **Las Ruinas del Teatro Brunet** at Calle Maceo 461. There's also a nightly salsa show in the courtyard of the **Casa de la Música** at Plaza Mayor.

In Remedios there are charming live band sessions at the **Kiosko Pando** in the centre of Parque Martí on Friday and Saturday nights.

Nightlife

In Cienfuegos **El Palatino** at 2514 Avenida 54 is a popular drinking spot with both locals and visitors; similarly the **Palacio de Valle** (▶ 104) offers an unusual mix of Cuban music and transvestite show, the performers in oriental clothing.

Two good bars in Camagüey are **El Cambio** on Calles Independencia and Martí, and the **Piano Bar** at the Gran Hotel on Calle Maceo (▶ 118).

In Trinidad visit **Taberna La Canchachara**, set in a 17th century colonial mansion - try the canchachara cocktail, made from local rum, lemon and honey.

In Remedios try **Taberna Don Juan** at 12 Calle Balmaceda or **El Louvre** at 122 Calle Máximo Gómez.

Nightlife at both Playa Ancón and Cayo Coco revolves around the large exclusive hotels, and is generally restricted to residents.

Discos

In Cienfuegos head out to **Discoteca El Benny Moré** at 2907 Avenida 54; alternatively La **Caribeña** on Calle 35 is an open-air disco enjoyed by both Cubans and tourists.

In Santa Clara the big disco scene is **Disco Villa Clara** at Parque Vidal 11. Catering mainly to young Cubans, its closed Mondays.

Camagüey's main disco is the **Sala de Fiesta Disco Café** at Calle Independencia 208.

Disco Ayala, set in a large cave behind Ermita de la Popa in Trinidad, is popular with visitors.

Larger hotels at beach resorts such as Cayo Coco and Playa

Ancón all have discotheques as part of their all-in entertainment scene, though these are almost always restricted to residents.

Music and Cabaret

In Cienfuegos the nearest you'll get to a cabaret show is the transvestite show at **Palacio de Valle** (▶ 121) – there are no large Tropicana-style nightspots in town.

In Trinidad there's a salsa show nightly in the courtyard of the **Casa de la Música** up the stairway by the Iglesia Parroquial de la Santísima Trinidad. Similarly at the **Taberna La Canchachara** on Rubén Martínez Villena at Ciro Redondo where good *salsa, sol* and other rhythms can be heard late into the night.

There's no formal cabaret show in Camagüey, but there is a show of a different kind every Saturday night. This is the celebrated *Noche Camagüeyana* or "Night of Camagüey". Locals and visitors come out to celebrate along a

stretch of Avenida República running south from the railway station. There are stalls selling food and alcohol, crowds of people dancing and sometimes a rock concert is held later in the evening.

Sports

Facilities for many kinds of **water-sports** exist at both Playa Ancón and Cayo Coco. These include swimming, snorkelling, diving, water-skiing and deep sea fishing. For details go to www.cubatravel.cu

Festivals

In Trinidad the *Fiestas Sanjuaneras* is a carnival that takes place over the last weekend of June. It's characterised by much singing, dancing and consumption of alcohol.

In Camagüey **carnival** is held each year during the last week of June. The *Jornadas de la Cultura Camagüeyana* celebrates the founding of the city and takes place during the first two weeks of February.

Eastern Cuba

Getting Your Bearings

Left: The road to the Sierra Maestra

Gibara

Holguín **6**

Eastern Cuba is quite different to the endless sugar fields of Central Cuba There are numerous mountain ranges such as the Sierra del Cristal near Holguín, the Sierra del Purial south of Baracoa, and the magnificent Sierra Maestra. Then there's the long Caribbean coast, heavily influenced by Cuba's second city, Santiago de Cuba.

R. Buey

5 □ Manzanillo

I Bayamo

R. Bayamo

CC

Further off the beaten track is the isolated and delightful old colonial town of Baracoa, Cuba's oldest European settlement. Dominated by the extraordinary flat-topped mountain El Yunque, and isolated from the rest of the country by high ranges of mountains, Baracoa is proud both of its age and of its distinctive cuisine – the only genuine regional cuisine in Cuba.

Other attractions include Cuba's fourth largest city, Holguín, with its fine late colonial period architecture, and Bayamo – perhaps the most charming provincial capital in Cuba, and revered nationally for its history as a centre of Cuban independence.

Eastern Cuba – Oriente – is different from the rest of the country. It feels closer to Jamaica and Haiti than to Havana (as indeed it is), and it is home to possibly the best musical rhythms, and certainly the most famous carnival, in the whole of Cuba.

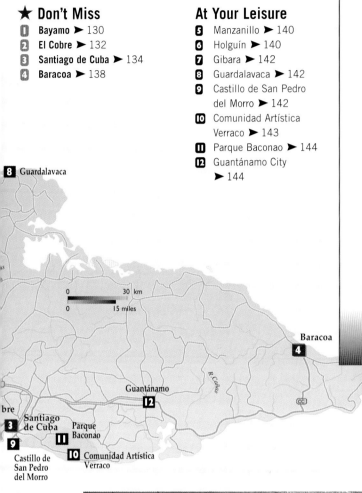

8 Guardalavaca

Baracoa
4

Guantánamo
12

bre
Santiago
3 de Cuba   Parque
9   Baconao
11
Castillo de   10 Comunidad Artística
San Pedro   Verraco
del Morro

0   30 km
0   15 miles

Page 125: An aspiring ballerina practices in the bandstand at Holguín's Parque Peralta
Right: Washing a horse in the river near Guantánamo City

The best way to travel round Eastern Cuba is by car or taxi with a driver. Start in Bayamo, then head east to explore Santiago de Cuba. From here it's a wonderful drive via Guantánamo to Baracoa, crossing the Sierra de Purial by a winding, switchback highway. On the fourth day head back from Baracoa northwest to Holguín. Finally, if you feel like sun, sea and sand, take a rest at the beach resort of Guardalavaca.

Eastern Cuba in Four Days

Day One

Morning
Make an early start and watch the women of **1 Bayamo** (➤ 130) washing and mopping Parque Céspedes while you have breakfast at the Royalton Hotel (➤ 145). Drive east along the *Carretera Central* for a snack and fuel in Contramaestre.

Afternoon
Continue your journey to **3 Santiago de Cuba** (➤ 134) via the old *Carretera Central* or join the southern spur of the *autopista* near Palma Soriano. Arrive in Santiago in the late afternoon.

Evening
Have drinks and dinner on the balcony of Hotel Casa Granda overlooking Parque Céspedes and Santiago Cathedral.

Day Two

Morning
Explore the heart of old Santiago by foot (➤ 162). Lunch at one of the restaurants on Plaza de Dolores.

Afternoon
Drive to **2 El Cobre** (➤ 132), returning via the eastern ring road in time to reach **9 Castillo de San Pedro del Morro** (➤ 142) by 6 pm. Watch the ceremonial firing of the cannon across the Bahía de Santiago at 7 pm.

Evening
Santiago has many restaurants and bars to choose from, as well as La Tropicana cabaret.

Day Three

Morning
Head southeast from Santiago de Cuba to
11 Parque Baconao (➤ 144), stopping at the
10 Comunidad Artística Verraco (➤ 143) en
route.

Afternoon
Drive to **12 Guantánamo City** (➤ 144) for snacks
and fuel. Continue to Cajobabo along the beautiful shore of the Caribbean, then swing inland
across the Sierra de Purial to **4 Baracoa**
(➤ 138), arriving in the late afternoon.

Evening
Have dinner and drinks – and maybe a cooling swim – at
Hotel El Castillo (➤ 145). Try the tempting *cocina
Baracoa* and watch the sun set behind El Yunque.

Day Four

Morning
Drive northwest along the Atlantic coast through the
foothills of the Alturas de Baracoa to the industrialised
town of Moa. From here continue to the small town of
Mayarí for a simple snack lunch of pizza.

Afternoon
Continue to **6 Holguín** (➤ 140) where you can book into a
hotel before heading north to the historic port of **7 Gibara**
(below, ➤ 142) where Christopher Columbus first made
landfall in Cuba. Alternatively, bypass Holguín and head
straight out to the beach resort of **8 Guardalavaca**
(➤ 142).

Evening
Drive out to the Mirador de Mayabe (➤ 147) near Holguín
or dine al fresco at the Atlantico in Guardalavaca.

Bayamo

Bayamo, founded in 1513, was one of the original seven towns established by the colonial pioneer Diego de Velázquez. It's probably the most attractive provincial capital in Eastern Cuba. With a population of around 120,000 it is both small and relaxed – which is of course a major part of its attraction.

The verdant peaks of the **Sierra Maestra** (➤ 166) dominate the landscape to the south, while a new ring road on the *Carretera Central* skirts well south of the town, leaving the historic town centre remarkably free of heavy traffic – though you will see plenty of horse-drawn carriages and, at weekends and during festivals, goat-drawn traps for children.

Catedral de Santísima Salvador

Life in Bayamo revolves around the extensive main square, **Parque Céspedes**. Bayamo was Carlos Manuel de Céspedes' birthplace and has a special place in the annals of Cuban patriotism. The Cuban national anthem, *La Bayamesa*, was also written here by **Perucho Figueredo** (1819–1870), another famous local citizen, during the anti-colonial wars of the 1860s. Figueredo was later captured and executed by the Spanish.

Heroes of Independence

Tall, shady trees dominate Parque Céspedes, a spotless square with a granite column bearing a bronze statue of Céspedes at its centre. Nearby another monument inscribed with the words of *La Bayamesa* bears a bust of Perucho Figueredo. On the park's north side, next to the restored Hotel Royalton, stands the **Casa Natal de Carlos Manuel de Céspedes**, now a museum. It's beautifully preserved and lovingly cared for by curators who clearly feel honoured by their task. Standing right next door is the Museo Colonial, which houses colonial period artefacts and the original script of *La Bayamesa*, is also well worth visiting.

On the east side of the square, in front of the attractive
Ayuntamiento or Town Hall, Céspedes proclaimed Cuba's
independence. It was also the site of the first Assembly of the
Cuban Republic.

A few short steps west of the park is another open square,
the **Plaza del Himno Nacional**, dominated by the **Catedral
de Santísima Salvador**. Dating from 1868 (when Bayamo
was rebuilt after being destroyed by fire), this splendid building features a mural above the altar showing Céspedes blessing the Cuban national flag.

TAKING A BREAK

The **Royalton Hotel** is stylish and overlooks Parque
Céspedes. It has two bars, one at ground level by the park,
providing excellent opportunities to sit, sip and quietly watch
the Bayamese go about their daily business. The second, on
the roof, gives fine views across the nearby cathedral to the
distant peaks of the Sierra Maestra.

🚹 184 B2
**Casa Natal de Carlos Manuel de
Céspedes**
✉ Calle Maceo 57, Parque
Céspedes 🕐 Tue–Sun 9–5
🎟 Inexpensive

Museo Colonial
✉ Calle Maceo 55, Parque
Céspedes 🕐 Tue–Fri 8–6, Sat–Sun
10–2
🎟 Inexpensive

Goat trap rides
for children

BAYAMO: INSIDE INFO

Top tip In the Plaza del Himno Nacional an old bar called **La Bodega** offers oys-
ter cocktails, a Bayamo delicacy.

Hidden gem Don't miss the **Capilla de la Dolorosa**, a small chapel dedicated to
the Virgin Mary on the west side of the Catedral de Santísima Salvador. This is
the only part of the original cathedral building to have survived the destruction
of 1868, and today it houses the **first flag of the Cuban Republic**, sewn by
Céspedes' wife. It's easy to see why Bayamo looms large in the Cuban national
consciousness.

❷ El Cobre

The Basilica de Nuestra Señora del Cobre, northwest of Santiago de Cuba on the old *Carretera Central* to Palma Soriano, is the most sacred Catholic religious site in Cuba and the nation's most popular and revered pilgrimage destination. It also has special significance to the Afro-Caribbean religion Santería (▶ 16).

Cobre means "copper" in Spanish, and it's easy to see where the name originates. El Cobre was the earliest open-cast copper mine in the Americas, and great piles of slag are visible in the area. But the real story of El Cobre goes back to 1606, when three fishermen sailing in the Bahía de Nipe, on the Atlantic coast, to the north of Santiago, recovered a floating Madonna from the waters. The 30-cm (11.7in) tall wooden image was of a *mestizo* (mixed race) Virgin Mary carrying the infant Christ in her left arm and holding a golden cross in her right hand. At her feet, in Spanish, was the inscription *Yo soy la Virgen de la Caridad*, or "I am the Virgin of Charity". Legend has it that the image had been floating for a hundred years, having been set adrift to protect it from the ill intentions of local idolatrous chieftains.

A new bride seeks a blessing at El Cobre

Cuba's Patron Saint

This miraculous figure was brought to El Cobre where the first sanctuary was erected in 1608. Ever since "Cachita" – as the image is known – was installed at El Cobre the people of the copper mines seemed to prosper. As her fame grew, so did her popularity, and in 1916 Pope Benedict proclaimed El Cobre's Virgin of Charity the patron saint of Cuba. The present, grand basilica that houses the virgin was inaugurated on her Saint's Day, 8 September, in 1927. Later, on the same day in 1936, her image was taken to Santiago de Cuba and formally crowned. As though to confirm the sanctification, Pope John Paul II performed a second coronation during his famous visit to Cuba in 1998.

The massive, cream-coloured basilica looks most impressive from the approach road. Inside, the arched nave is simple and certainly not overly ornate, but there's no mis-

taking the dedication of the pilgrims and devotees who crowd around the tiny figure of the Virgin, dressed in a yellow-coloured, gold-encrusted gown and wearing a replica of her crown. The image is housed behind glass on an upper floor behind the main altar where supplicants kneel seeking blessings, cures, or giving thanks for prayers already answered.

Above: The Basilica de Nuestra Señora del Cobre

Left: "Cachita" – Cuba's patron saint

Tens of thousands of worshippers visit El Cobre every 8 September, Catholic and Santería devotees mingling and mixing both physically and spiritually. It's no coincidence that the Virgin wears yellow – the colour of the Santería *orisha* Ochún, the sensual Yoruba (West African) goddess of love, rhythm, dance and rivers.

TAKING A BREAK

There are no special restaurants or *miradors* (viewpoints) serving drinks on the winding road between Santiago and El Cobre. Visit the basilica and then head back to Santiago to relax.

➕ 184 C2 ✉ 21km (13 miles) northwest of Santiago de Cuba 🕐 Daily 6:30–6 💲 Free

EL COBRE: INSIDE INFO

Top tips Religious **mementoes** are readily available at numerous souvenir shops throughout the small town.

• Locals will approach you and try to sell small pieces of discarded **low-grade copper ore** which is supposedly lucky.

③ Santiago de Cuba

Cuba's second city is the country's most important regional centre. An ancient township, established in 1514 by the conquistador Diego de Velázquez, it has a rich cultural history and intellectual tradition. It's also the first city of the Cuban Revolution; it was here that Fidel Castro mounted his initial, failed attack on the Moncada Barracks in 1953, and here that he eventually declared the triumph of the revolution in 1959.

Santiago faces the Caribbean culturally as well as geographically, and is very different to distant Havana. The roots of its rich culture are founded in the diversity of its inhabitants, a Cuban melting pot comprising Spanish, French and Afro-Caribbean peoples who have lived side-by-side, influencing each other's music, song, dance, literature and art to the extent that the resulting mix has become a distinctively *Santiaguero* whole. There's no other city in Cuba with quite the joyous rhythm of life of Santiago de Cuba, and this is particularly true during the summer when one festival seems to follow another.

Narrow Alleys

Old Santiago is a warren of narrow streets and alleys sloping gently downhill from **Plaza de Marte** eastwards to the Bahía de Santiago and the Caribbean Sea (➤ 162). The most important buildings in this ancient heart of the city are clustered around **Parque Céspedes** and include the fine neo-classical **Ayuntamiento** or Town Hall, the venerable **Casa de Velázquez**, dating from 1522 and said to be the oldest surviving building in Cuba – it now houses the **Museo de Ambiente Histórico Cubano**, featuring period antiques dating from the 16th to 19th centuries; and the **Hotel Casa Granda** (➤ 146) with its wonderful first-floor terrace bar. The square is dominated by Santiago's most important building, the **Catedral de Nuestra Señora de la Asunción**, a five-century old church, frequently restored, which dates back to the time of Diego de Velázquez who is also believed to be entombed somewhere here.

Other significant squares in the old quarter include **Plaza de Dolores** and **Plaza de Marte**, both within comfortable walking distance. Santiago is a sizeable city, and there's plenty to see beyond its historic heart.

Northwest of the centre is the **Cementerio Santa Ifigenia**, the resting place of many of Santiago's – and Cuba's – finest and bravest heroes. Here you will find the imposing hexagonal Mausoleum of the nation's father, José Martí (1853–95); the grave of Tomás Estrada Palma (1835–1908), Cuba's first president; and the tomb of the father of Cuban independence, Carlos Manuel de Céspedes (1819–74). Many of the graves in the cemetery are those of independence fighters killed in the colonial wars of independence against Spain, while more recent revolutionary heroes, including victims of the Batista dictatorship, are also interred here.

Above: Visitors at the Casa de las Religiones Populares
Left: The Monumento Maceo, dedicated to independence hero General Antonio Maceo

Birthplace of the Revolution

About 2km (1.2 miles) east, along the major thoroughfare Paseo de Martí, a small side road, Calle Moncada, leads to the former **Moncada Barracks**, site of Fidel Castro's first strike against Batista in 1953 and now a school – though the walls are still riddled, in places, with bullet holes serving as reminders of the great event.

West of Moncada the main highway Avenida Victoriano Garzón leads to Avenida de los Américas and the vast **Plaza de la Revolución**. This is the heart of revolutionary Santiago, dominated by the huge **Monumento Maceo**, an equestrian statue of the legendary general who led the resistance against the Spanish colonial presence in Oriente for many years.

Historic buildings and revolutionary monuments aside, Santiago has its share of more esoteric attractions. For those who can't make it to the Grand Carnival in July, the **Museo del Carnaval** on Calle Heredia in the heart of the old city has displays of carnival dress, floats and related photographs. Nearby on Bartolomé Masó the **Museo del Ron** (Museum of Rum) offers tribute to yet another of Cuba's celebrated indulgences. Also associated with rum, or at least the profits derived from it, the **Museo Emilio Bacardí Moreau** on Calle Pío Rosado is Santiago's best museum, as well as Cuba's oldest. It was founded in 1899 by rum millionaire Emilio Bacardí y Moreau and contains many fine examples of Cuban art, from pre-Columbian Indian artefacts, through memorabilia (including weapons, flags and maps) from Cuba's long wars of independence from Spain, to paintings from some of the nation's most distinguished artists. All three museums are within comfortable strolling distance of the central Plaza de Dolores.

Further Afield

Other museums worth visiting can be found further out of town to the east, beyond Parque Ferreiro. This is too far to walk comfortably, and it's better to take a taxi. Here, on the small side road Calle 5, off Avenida Manduley, is the **Centro Cultural Africano Fernando Ortiz**, with a collection of artefacts from Africa. At Manduley Calle 13, the **Casa de las Religiones Populares**, a museum devoted to the religion of Santería (► 16), has many interesting and unusual artefacts associated with this Afro-Caribbean cult. Almost next door – to the north, but also on Calle 13 – is the **Casa del Caribe**, a small institution founded in 1982 to study Caribbean life and culture. This organisation arranges the annual Festival of Caribbean Culture which takes place in early July, as well as teaching short courses on aspects of Afro-Cuban music, dance and popular religion.

Right: Tomb of José Martí, Cementerio Santa Ifigenia

Left: Getting ready for Carnival

TAKING A BREAK

It's difficult to beat the laid-back, shady atmosphere of **La Taberna de Dolores** (► 148) on the south side of Plaza de Dolores. Popular with young Cubans, there's draught beer, live music, good food and a friendly atmosphere.

Santiago de Cuba 137

🞤 185 D2

Museo de Ambiente Histórico Cubano
🞤 186 B3
✉ Parque Céspedes
☎ (22) 652-652
🕐 Mon–Sat 9–5, Sun 9–1
🛈 Moderate

Museo del Ron
🞤 186 C3
✉ Calle Bartolomé Masó 358
🕐 Mon–Fri 9–5, Sat 9–1
🛈 Inexpensive

Museo Emilio Bacardí Moreau
🞤 186 C3
✉ Calle Pío Rosado, just off Aguilera
☎ (22) 628-402
🕐 Daily 10–8
🛈 Moderate

Museo del Carnaval
🞤 186 C3
✉ Calle Heredia 340
☎ (22) 626-955
🕐 Tue–Sun 9–5
🛈 Inexpensive

SANTIAGO DE CUBA: INSIDE INFO

Top tips Santiago's two most significant festivals are the **Festival of Caribbean Culture** in early July and the two-week-long **Grand Carnival** in late July. Throughout this period carnival dance troupes known as *comparsas* compete with each other and the whole city celebrates with a non-stop festival of *son*, *salsa*, *mambo*, *conga* and *cha-cha-chá*.
• Santiago de Cuba is a major fishing port. Good seafood isn't always easy to come by in Cuba, so if you get a chance to eat freshly fried fish, or better yet **fresh lobster** while in Santiago, seize it at once.

4 Baracoa

Relatively few visitors will make it to remote Baracoa near the island's easternmost tip, which is a pity, as this town is one of Cuba's most interesting spots. It isn't nearly as isolated as it once was, until the 1960s, before the building of the highway that cuts north through the mountainous Sierra de Purial from the Caribbean at Cajobabo, the only way to visit Baracoa was by sea.

Today Baracoa is a delightful old town of around 50,000 inhabitants. Founded in 1512 by Diego de Velázquez it predates both Havana and Santiago de Cuba, making it the oldest colonial town in Cuba. It's possible, as the inhabitants will tell you, that this is where Christopher Columbus first made landfall on the island in 1492. His journals describe landing on a headland between two bays on "the most beautiful land man's eyes have ever seen", and he mentions a flat-topped mountain dominating the area. Baracoans agree that this is a reference to **El Yunque** (The Anvil), a massive peak just northeast of town. The people of Gibara (► 142), as well as most historians, would beg to differ, however, and claim that Columbus first made landfall there.

A Town of Fortresses

Either way, Baracoa is steeped in history. It has three Spanish forts, all designed to keep English raiders at bay, but none able to do so. Today the main fort, **El Castillo de Serboruco** (1740), dominates the town and has been converted into one of the most attractive and exclusive hotels in Cuba. Of the two other forts, **Fuerte Matachín** (1802) stands at the southern entrance to town by the Bahía de Miel (Bay of Honey) and is now the **Museo Municipal**, while **Fuerte de la Punta** (1803) which once guarded the southern entrance to Baracoa's magnificent harbour, the Bahía de Baracoa, is now a restaurant.

Baracoa Bay and harbour

Other attractions include the **Catedral de Nuestra Señora de la Asunción**, which dates from 1833. It's located on the southern side of Parque Central. Outside, in the park facing the church, is the bust of Hatuey, the famous Indian resistance leader, burned by the Spanish at this spot more than 500 years ago. Inside is the pride and joy of Baracoa – the **Cruz de la Parra**, said to have been raised by Columbus in 1492 and now bound in silver and carefully protected in a glass case. Carbon dating places the cross back to the 15th century, though the wood used is of Cuban and not Spanish origin. It may be necessary to enter the church through a small side door, on the western side of the building, as the main entrance is often barred.

For a drink or a meal overlooking the Bahía de Miel try **Hotel La Rusa** on the seafront. First established by Magdalena Rovieskuya, a Russian refugee described in Alejo Carpentier's *La Consagracion de la Primavera* (The Consecration of Spring), Errol Flynn, Fidel Castro and Che Guevara are all said to have stayed here.

🚩 185 F2

Museo Municipal
✉ Fuerte Matachín, Calle José Martí
🕐 Daily 8–6
💲 Inexpensive

BARACOA: INSIDE INFO

Top tips Don't miss **Baracoa's regional cuisine**. *La cocina Baracoa* (➤ 41) is spicier than elsewhere in the country and utilises coconut milk, cocoa, annatto seeds to colour rice yellow, and more garlic and fresh lime than is usual in standard *cocina criolla*.

• A noisy, **fun-filled carnival** takes place along Baracoa's seafront in early April.

At Your Leisure

5 Manzanillo

This sleepy fishing port feels a long way from anywhere, but is worth a visit – especially when taking the long drive around the Sierra Maestra (► 166). Manzanillo lives chiefly off the sea. The waters of the Golfo de Guacanayabo lap the town's all-but-deserted Malecón and are a prime source of crab, shrimp and lobster; a large proportion of Cuba's commercial fishing vessels are based here.

Manzanillo has few visitors, and as a consequence, almost everything is priced in non-convertible pesos. The port is still worth a visit, chiefly for the central Parque Céspedes, distinguished by some unexpected and rather lovely Moorish-style architecture. Best is the central *kiosko* or bandstand, along with various other buildings scattered around the square. The architect may have been inspired by thoughts of Seville, but clearly wasn't an Arab – the "Arabic script" on the *kiosko* isn't real Arabic at all, but still adds an unexpected Andalucian Islamic element to this remote corner of Cuba.

The Malecón is also worth a visit. Well-executed reclining figures in stone decorate the seafront in apparently random places, and there are peso rum and beer bars where you can sit and gaze across the azure Caribbean.

🚹 184 B2 ✉ 65km (40 miles) west of Bayamo

6 Holguín

With a population of 250,000, this is Cuba's fourth largest city and a good

Holguín from the Spanish in 1872. The **Museo de Historia Provincial** explains this and other local history. Also known as the "Parrot Cage" because it was once guarded by Spanish colonial troops who wore elaborate green, yellow and red uniforms, the most important exhibit is a fine pre-Columbian axe-head carved to resemble an Indian head. It's known as the *Hacha de Holguín* (Holguín Axe) and is an important provincial symbol.

Further south still is Parque Peralta, perhaps the most attractive of Holguín's civic squares, dominated by the early 18th-century Catedral de San Isidoro and boasting an attractive central *kiosko* or bandstand where local children sometimes practice dancing.

The countryside around Holguín can be truly lovely, and perhaps the best views of all are from the Mirador de Mayabe, 8km (5 miles) southeast of town. There are restaurant and hotel facilities near the *mirador*.

✚ 184 C3

Museo de Historia Provincial

✉ Calle Frexes 198 ☎ (24) 463-395 🕐 Mon–Sat 9–5

✋ Inexpensive

The Moorish *kiosko*, Parque Céspedes, Manzanillo

Catedral de San Isidoro in Holguín

place to stop overnight, with a number of hotels and restaurants. Within the city there are three centrally located parks. To the north is Parque Céspedes with early 19th-century Iglesia de San José at its centre.

Of more interest and just to the south is Parque Calixto García, centred on a statue of General García who liberated

7 Gibara

The small port of Gibara, on Cuba's Atlantic coast, is probably the site of Columbus' first landing on the island – despite the protests of outraged Baracoans (► 138). It makes a good side trip from either Holguín or Guardalavaca, perhaps for a seafood meal, a stroll along the Malecón, and a look at the statue of Christopher Columbus on the west side of the shallow Río Cacoyugüín where it empties into the sea.

The port is chiefly notable for its colonial architecture, and the fine views of town and bay from the crumbling fort at El Cuartelón, an old Spanish garrison on Los Caneyes Hill overlooking the town from the west.

➕ 184 C4 ✉ 35km (21.7 miles) north of Holguín

8 Guardalavaca

This is another of Socialist Cuba's "all in" package resorts, though it is possible to find both independent accommodation and restaurants. There's a long, powdery, white sand beach, warm sea and numerous water sports opportunities including snorkelling, scuba-diving, deep-sea fishing, windsurfing, sailing and kayaking. An attractive coral reef lies just 250m (275 yards) offshore.

The downside, as with most other, similarly exclusive government-run resorts, is that it's a long way from anywhere, and it's expensive (US$40 dollars minimum) to take a taxi to Holguín or Gibara.

➕ 185 D4 ✉ 54km (33.5 miles) northeast of Holguín

9 Castillo de San Pedro del Morro

This is one of the great sights of Oriente – and if you can arrange to be there around 7pm it's also one of the most spectacular. This impressive fortress – generally known as **El Morro** for short – was built by the Spanish in the mid-17th century to protect the Bahía de Santiago from pirates and, subsequently, from the British. The great bastions and

Strolling the beach at Playa Guardalavaca

crenellated walls completely dominate the entrance to Santiago harbour from the east, and are in excellent condition. El Morro is generally considered the best-preserved Spanish military fortification in the Caribbean, and is a UNESCO World Cultural Heritage Site.

A tour of the castle includes visits to the dungeons, bastions and batteries, but the highlight has to be each evening at 7 pm, when a squad of Cuban soldiers, dressed in the uniform of the independence fighters who liberated the island from Spain, march into the castle with great ceremony. The Cuban flag is raised, a genuine 18th-century cannon is loaded, the old-fashioned way, with gunpowder, a coir missile, and discharged across the bay with a powder fuse. A great cry of *Viva Cuba Libre!* (Long Live Free Cuba) goes up from the soldiers, and the ceremony is over. It's a sight well worth seeing, strongly evocative of former times.

➕ 185 D2 ✉ 10km (6.2 miles) southwest of Santiago de Cuba ⏰ Mon–Fri 9–7:30 Sat–Sun 8–7:30 💰 Moderate

🔟 Comunidad Artística Verraco

Southeast of Santiago the road to Baconao passes a small artists community called Comunidad Artística Verraco. In this isolated spot about a dozen individuals have set up workshops producing ceramics, wood carvings, paintings, iron work and a range of unusual artefacts. The community, which nestles beneath the high Gran Piedra range, is located 2km (1.2 miles) after El Verraco on the road to Baconao. Visitors (and customers in particular) are most welcome. About 10km (6.2 miles) before El Verraco on the left (north) side of the road a good route leads to the summit of La Gran Piedra, offering fantastic views across the Caribbean as well as a variety of refreshments.

🞧 185 D2 ✉ 34km (22 miles) southeast of Santiago de Cuba 🕐 Daily 8–7

Castillo de San Pedro del Morro

⑪ Parque Baconao

This is a popular day trip for *Santiagueros*, and a good place to take the children. There's a pleasant beach with a diving platform at Playa

Siboney, then the road winds eastwards through pleasant countryside to the Valle de la Prehistoria, a fantastic theme park devoted to life-size dinosaurs and prehistoric man. It's well done, and combined with the beach makes a pleasant day's outing.

✚ 185 D2

Valle de la Prehistoria
✉ 28km (17.4 miles) southeast of Santiago de Cuba ⓒ Daily 7:30–6:30 ✋ Moderate

⑫ Guantánamo City

Guantánamo is more famous for its bay, home to the large US naval and airbase, than for anything the city itself

A roadside vendor in Guantánamo City

has to offer. Sometimes it's possible to view the base from raised platforms at **Caimanera** to the west of the bay, or from **Mirador de Malones** to the east. Direct access to the base, isolated from the rest of Cuba by the largest minefield in the western hemisphere, is quite impossible. Guantánamo City is best considered as a refreshment stop on the rewarding drive from Santiago de Cuba to Baracoa. Parque Martí, in the centre of the city, has a couple of peso restaurants and a small but attractive church, the Parroquia de Sante Catalinia de Riccis (1862).

✚ 185 E2

Caimanera
✉ 21km (13 miles) south of Guantánamo City ⓒ Daily 9–5 ✋ Moderate

Mirador de Malones
✉ 27km (16.7 miles) southeast of Guantánamo City to the Cuban military checkpoint, then 15km (9.3 miles) to viewpoint ⓒ Daily 9–5 ✋ Expensive

Left: Valle de la Prehistoria at Parque Baconao

Where to... Stay

Prices
Expect to pay per double room per night
$ under US$50 $$ US$50–150 $$$ over US$150

BARACOA

El Castillo $$

This is an exceptionally good hotel by provincial Cuban standards, and would qualify as up-market anywhere in the Caribbean. Set in Baracoa's largest and highest fortress, El Castillo de Seboruco, the foundations of the hotel date from 1739 and offer wonderful views east, across the Bahía de Miel, north across the Bahía de Baracoa and Baracoa Harbour, and west to the "table mountain" of Baracoa, El Yunque. Amenities include a fine swimming pool between the hotel, the open-air bar and the air-conditioned restaurant. The latter offers some of the best Baracoan cuisine (▶ 139) in town. Other facilities include a souvenir shop and secure parking on the hill top outside the fort. Certainly the best place to stay in Baracoa, if not in the whole of Oriente.

➕ 185 F2 🖾 Loma del Paraíso, Calixto García ☎ (21) 42125; fax: (21) 355519

La Rusa $

Another notable hotel, pleasantly situated on Baracoa's quiet Malecón. The restaurant is fine; the rooms clean but basic and the prices reasonable. Yet it's the hotel's history, rather than its location and facilities, which give added appeal. The hotel was established by Magdalena Rovieskuya, a Russian woman whose image hangs in the lobby. According to some she was a Russian aristocrat who fled the revolution and retired to Baracoa where she continued to wear Russian court dress under a burning Cuban sun. Others suggest she simply tired of Stalinist Russia and took the opportunity to move to the tropics. Either way, her legend contributes to the appeal of Hotel La Rusa, not least because she features in Alejo Carpentier's Cuban novel *La Consagración de la Primavera*. Other famous guests who have stayed here are said to include Errol Flynn, Fidel Castro and Ernesto "Che" Guevara.

➕ 185 F2 🖾 Calle Máximo Gómez 161, Malecón ☎ (21) 43011

BAYAMO

Royalton $

Well positioned on the north side of Parque Céspedes, the renovated colonial-style Royalton is top of the range for Bayamo and very pleasant, though not unreasonably expensive. There's a relaxing sidewalk terrace where you can sit, sip and watch the Bayamese go about their business. There's also a rooftop bar with views across the square to the distant but imposing Sierra Maestra. At weekends and during festivals the locals organise goat-trap rides for children in the street outside.

➕ 184 B2 🖾 Calle Antonio Maceo 53 ☎ (23) 422290; fax: (23) 424792

GUARDALAVACA

Atlantico $$

A large complex catering for everyone from package tourists to independent travellers set right by the sea. Amenities include restaurants, bars, a large swimming pool, car rentals and money exchange. Unusually for Cuba – at least away from Varadero and the main all-in resorts – there's a children's programme, while for the adults there's a Marlin scuba-diving centre. Trips to Holguín or Gibara can be arranged by taxi, though the fares are pretty steep by Cuban standards. This is really a place to lay back and relax rather than a base for exploring the surrounding countryside.

➕ 185 D4 ⊠ Playa Guardalavaca, Banes ☎ (24) 30180; fax: (24) 30200

HOLGUÍN

El Bosque $

About 5km east of the town centre, this is more of a motel than hotel, with 70 small bungalows, a swimming pool, a bar and a restaurant. It's convenient if you're driving yourself, avoiding the narrow streets of Holguín and providing safe parking. At weekends there's a disco by the pool, but because the bungalows are fairly spread out the noise problem isn't too bad.

➕ 184 C3 ⊠ Avenida Jorge Dimitrov, Reparto Pedro Díaz Cello ☎ (24) 481012; fax: (24) 481140

Pernik $

This is Holguín's inevitable Soviet-era giant – not terribly attractive architecturally, but with easily the best facilities in Holguín, ranging from shops and money-changing services to a pharmacy and (at least notionally) medical attention. The first-floor restaurant serves the large *criollo* buffet meals, and there's also a smaller 24-hour cafeteria beside the large swimming pool that serves good pizza and tasty spaghetti at very reasonable prices. As usual, it can be noisy at weekends when disco music blares out by the poolside until around 10 pm. If this bothers you, ask for a room in the eastern wing.

➕ 184 C3 ⊠ Avenida Jorge Dimitrov and Plaza de la Revolución ☎ (24) 481011; fax: (24) 481667

SANTIAGO DE CUBA

Balcón de Caribe $

This is a very pleasant place to stay – it's quiet, there's no problem parking and you're close by the historic castle of El Morro and the attractive southern reaches of the Bahía Santiago de Cuba. There's a choice of simple but clean and comfortable hotel rooms or individual bunga-lows, plus a swimming pool, two bars and a restaurant. Next door is the Cabaret San Pedro del Mar, with an elaborate floorshow nightly.

➕ 185 D2 ⊠ 10km (6.5 miles) south of town, Carretera del Morro km7.5 ☎ (22) 691011; fax: (22) 692398

Casa Granda $$

The best hotel in Santiago de Cuba, with a superb location overlooking Parque Céspedes and the Catedral de Nuestra Señora de la Asunción. Set in a fine old colonial building, this establishment has been fully renovated and is now under joint Cuban-French management – and this certainly shows in the superior quality of the place. The rooms are tastefully furnished in period style and there's a wonderful patio-style lobby bar overlooking the square which serves good meals. For something more up-market (and definitely more expensive) there's the elegant Restaurante Casa Granda. There are also parking facilities – essential for downtown Santiago with its narrow streets and pedestrianised squares.

➕ 186 C3 ⊠ Calle Heredia 201, between Lacret and San Félix ☎ (22) 686600; fax: (22) 686035

Libertad $

One of the best places to stay in town – though parking nearby can be a problem. The rooms are clean and reasonably priced, service is of an almost old world courtesy – the maids arrange bath towels to resemble swans or flowers when they make up the room each morning, and leave notes wishing you a "good day". There's a relaxing bar, a tasty *criollo* restaurant and – most unusual outside Havana – an email café that functions sometimes.

➕ 186 D3 ⊠ Calle Aguilera 658, Plaza de Marte ☎ (22) 623080

Where to...
Eat and Drink

Prices

Expect to pay per person for a two-course meal, excluding drinks and service

$ under US$10 $$ US$10–25 $$$ over US$25

BARACOA

El Castillo $$

If you're looking for style and comfort in Baracoa, then it's difficult to go wrong with El Castillo – indeed there are few other even moderately good restaurants in town, so this is both the place to stay and the place to eat. Baracoa is unusual as it's the only town in Cuba with a distinctive (if fairly simple) regional cuisine (▶ 139). You can dine here on coconut rice and spicy stewed chicken or other local delicacies. The restaurant is air-conditioned and there's live music most evenings. Afterwards it's pleasant to have a nightcap in the poolside bar with fine views across the dimly lit town and harbour far below.

🚹 185 F2 ⊠ Loma del Paraíso, Calixto García ☎ (21) 42125; fax: (21) 355519 ⏰ Daily 11:30–2, 6–10

La Colonial $

A small but elegant local restaurant offering Baracoa cuisine and other criollo fare. Portions are generous and the service good. The house speciality is seafood, especially prawns and lobster, though swordfish is also generally on the menu.

🚹 184 B2 ⊠ Calle General García

In eastern Cuba the standard Moros y Christianos (black beans and rice) is often replaced with congri, or rice and red kidney beans. If this doesn't suit, there's always papas fritas to fall back on!

🚹 185 F2 ⊠ Calle José Martí 123 and Calle Frank País ☎ (21) 43161 ⏰ Daily 6 pm–10 pm

BAYAMO

Restaurante 1513 $

This is the largest of Bayamo's state-run restaurants, though not as good as the more appealing Restaurant Hotel Royalton. But if you're staying in Bayamo for more than a couple of days and you feel like a change, this is the place to go. The simple criollo menu features all the usual dishes (subject to availability), grilled chicken, pork steaks, spaghetti, pizza – generally served with congri (red kidney beans and rice) rather than Moros y Christianos (black beans and rice).

🚹 184 B2 ⊠ Calle General García

176 and Calle Lora ☎ (23) 422921 ⏰ Daily 11:30–2, 6–10

HOLGUÍN

Mirador de Mayabe $$

The hotel at Villa Mirador de Mayabe has a pretty good thatched restaurant serving local Cuban fare but offering really fantastic views across the hills and valleys of Holguín Province. The mirador or viewpoint is the real attraction, but the grilled fish and papas fritas are good. Try the local Holguín-brewed Mayabe beer, which is full-bodied but at 3.8 per cent less alcoholic than Bucanero.

🚹 184 C3 ⊠ Alturas de Mayabe Km8 ☎ (24) 422160 ⏰ Daily 11:30–2:30, 5:30–9:30

Taberna Pancho $

A good, cheap place to eat between Hotel Pernik and Motel El Bosque to the east of town. It caters mainly for locals paying in non-convertible pesos, but dollar guests are most welcome and get priority treatment, with no waiting. The food is standard Cuban fare – hamburger, *papas fritas* and Mayabe beer make a good if simple meal. If you're in luck there will be some Tabasco sauce or salsa to perk up the flavour.

➕ 184 C3 ☒ Avenida Jorge Dimitrov ☎ (24) 481868 ⏱ Daily noon–4, 6–10

SANTIAGO DE CUBA

El Cayo $$

This is a great place to go towards sunset. It's set on the small island of Cayo Granma in Santiago de Cuba Bay – you must take a ferry from Ciudamar on the Carretera del Morro – and has fantastic views across the bay towards the impressive medieval castle of El Morro. At 7 pm you will clearly hear the evening cannon being fired. The house speciality is seafood, and it doesn't get much better than this. Grilled lobster and prawn paella top the menu.

➕ 185 D2 ☒ Cayo Granma ☎ (22) 690109 ⏱ Daily noon–2, 6–9:30

El Morro $$

A little more up-market and more expensive than El Cayo, this is perhaps the best restaurant on the outskirts of Santiago de Cuba. Perched on the clifftops just east of El Morro, the restaurant has really good views across the Caribbean. It's decorated in a studiously rustic style and guests can eat inside or on the attractive patio terrace. The menu is a mix of *criollo* fare and international cuisine, with two different varieties of bean soup and baked fish with prawns and garlic as the recommended house dishes.

➕ 185 D2 ☒ Near the entrance to the castle, Carretera del Morro ☎ (22) 691576 ⏱ Daily noon–9

La Perla del Dragon $$

A Sino-Cuban establishment offering dishes with at least a Chinese flavour about them – sweet and sour pork or spring rolls are the usual standbys, with chop suey a close third. Still, if you want a change from *criollo* fare, however unlikely the claims to be Chinese may seem, this is the place to go in Santiago de Cuba. The setting is pleasant – Plaza de Dolores is the city's most relaxed and attractive square – and the service is friendly and fairly prompt.

➕ 186 C3 ☒ Calles Aguilera and Calvario, Plaza de Dolores ☎ (22) 652307 ⏱ Daily 11:30–2:30, 6:30–11

La Taberna de Dolores $

Perhaps the best place to eat in Santiago – certainly the atmosphere is extremely friendly, with live music, and the narrow inner courtyard with shady trees and terraces is both cool and intimate. Lots of young Cubans come here to hang out and drink draught beer, but the food is pretty good too – especially the grilled fish, and perhaps the most succulent *congri* (red kidney beans and rice) in Oriente. Prices are very reasonable, the staff friendly but sometimes overworked. Don't expect fast service; this is a place to relax.

➕ 186 C3 ☒ Calle Aguilera 468 and Plaza de Dolores ☎ (22) 623913 ⏱ Daily 11 am–1 am

Zun Zun $$

An elegant and fairly expensive restaurant located in the western suburbs of Vista Alegre, beyond Parque Ferreiro. The cuisine in mixed Cuban-Spanish-international and dishes to look out for include char-grilled lobster, shrimp paella and barbecued chicken. If you're eating *criollo* then try the tender and nourishing *congri* and – when available – the *yuca con mojo* (cassava cooked in garlic sauce). There's a limited wine list, and the selection of beers should include the local Hatuey brand (5.4 per cent) brewed in Santiago de Cuba since the 1920s.

➕ 185 D2 ☒ Avenida Manduley 159, Reparto Vista Alegre ☎ (22) 641528 ⏱ Mon–Sat noon–10, Sun noon–3

Where to...
Shop

Souvenirs

With the single exception of Santiago de Cuba, Oriente is not particularly rich in souvenir shops. **Holguín** is a sizeable town but sees few tourists and has little to offer. **Bayamo** is rather better, despite its smaller size, and has a pedestrian shopping zone south of Parque Céspedes along **Calle General García**. Guantánamo City has almost no tourist traffic, and it's only at the few major beach resorts – **Guardalavaca** being the largest – that government-owned hotels run small souvenir shops selling T-shirts, a handful of books and assorted knick-knacks like maracas and Che Guevara badges or berets.

Santiago de Cuba is another matter. This large city is geared up for tourism, especially during carnival (▶ 137). Souvenirs and local handicrafts are readily available at **Cuba Artesanía**, Calle Félix Peña 673, near the Casa de Nuestra Señora de la Asunción. **La Maison**, at Avenida Manduley 52 in the richer eastern suburbs of the city, sells imported and up-market clothing. A branch of the government-owned **Artex** chain at the Casa de la Trova, Calle Heredia 208, sells many souvenirs including local *Santiaguero* music on tapes and CDs. If you're interested in music, the **Fábrica de Instrumentos Musicales Sindo Garay** at Calle Patricio Lumumba 53 sells guitars, maracas, drums and other instruments.

Arts and Crafts

Santiago de Cuba is an arts centre second in importance only to Havana. It's different, too, in that the arts scene is notably less Hispanic and more Caribbean. **Galería de Arte de Oriente** at Calle General Lacret 656 between Calles Heredia and Aguilera is just one of several galleries in the Heredia area. Another noteworthy outlet for paintings and sculptures is **Galería Santiago** on the south side of Parque Céspedes by the Cathedral. **Arte Universal** on Calle 1, between Calles M and Terazza, just north of the Hotel Las Américas, is a gallery selling paintings. It also puts on daily art exhibitions except Mondays.

Bayamo has less of an arts scene, but **Fondo de Bienes Culturales** in the centre of town, sells local handicrafts and sculptures, while **Galería Provincial** at Calle General García 174 displays and sells the work of local artists.

Holguín has a **Fondo de Bienes Culturales** at Calle Frexes 196 by Parque Calixto García. **Galería Holguín** at Calle Manduley 137 sells local artwork, as does the **Artex Tienda Holguín** at Frexes 236. If you go along to the **Mercado Artesanal** at 91 Martí on Parque Calixto García you can watch local painters at work as well as viewing paintings for sale. In Baracoa, check out the shops at **Hotel El Castillo**.

Imported Goods

All the provincial capitals of the Eastern region including **Las Tunas, Holguín, Bayamo, Santiago de Cuba** and **Guantánamo City** have branches of the hard-currency chain **Tiendas Panamericanas**. These are just about the only place to stock up on imported foodstuffs or toiletries. On longer drives its best to purchase snacks and bottled water in centres like **Santiago de Cuba**, **Holguín** and **Bayamo**. The same is true of any pharmaceutical items you may require. It's also very important to keep an eye on the fuel gauge – in Oriente it can sometimes be 100km (64 miles) or more between petrol or diesel stations, and it's all too easy to run out of fuel. The only other locations to find imported goods are at all-in resorts in places like **Guardalavaca** and **Marea de Portillo**.

Where to...
Be Entertained

Most of Eastern Cuba offers limited artistic and cultural entertainment, but vibrant Santiago de Cuba more than makes up for this, fairly bursting with artistic, musical and cultural energy – not to mention Carnival. Most tourist hotels have bars and other in-house entertainment.

The Arts

Bayamo presents theatrical performances at the **Sala Teatro José Joaquín Palma** in the old church at Calle Cespédes 164; they also give children's shows on Saturday and Sunday mornings at 10 am. Highly recommended are the Cuban folk singing performances held at the **Casa de la Trova La Bayamesa** at the junction of Calles Maceo and Martí.

Holguín's main theatre, the **Teatro Commandante Eddy Suñol** on Parque Calixto García, features regular comic opera and ballet performances. Traditional Cuban folk music can be heard at the **Casa de la Trova** at Calle Maceo 174 (closed on Monday). Right next door at Calle Maceo 172, the **Casa de la Cultura** features art exhibitions and performances of classical music.

Santiago de Cuba's **Teatro Heredia** at the junction of Avenida de las Américas and Avenida de los Desfiles stages everything from classical concerts to rock music. The **Sala de Conciertos Esteban Salas** at the junction of Calles Aguilera and Mayía Rodriguez, by contrast, is purely classical. The **Sala Teatro El Mambí** at Calle Bartolomé Masó 303 has puppet shows at weekends.

Nightlife

Bayamo is a quiet town, but visitors can get a shot of rum at the **Café Oriente** on Parque Cespédes or an iced beer or cocktail at **Hotel Royalton** (▶ 145). In Holguín **Bar La Malagueña** at Calle Martí 129 is a popular standby. Rather more down-market is **El Coctelito** at Calle Manduley 153.

Nightlife in Santiago is jumping. One excellent bar is the **Taberna de Dolores** (▶ 148); also the **Claqueta Bar La Peña** 654, **Club 300** at Calle Aguilera 302, and **Bar Terraza Mirador** at Calle Hartmann 658.

Discos

There's just one disco in Bayamo – **Disco Bayamesa** in the Hotel Sierra Maestra 3km (2 miles) southeast of town on the *Carretera Central* to Santiago de Cuba.

Holguín's main dance club is **Disco Cristal** at Calle Manduley 199. Other places include **Disco La Roca** at the junction of Calles Maceo and Urbano. There's also a disco every night at **Hotel Pernik** (▶ 146).

Santiago de Cuba has lots of dance clubs and discos. Among the best are **Club El Iris** at Calle Aguilera 617, the rooftop disco **La Melipona** by the Hotel Las Américas, and **Discoteca Espanta Sueño** at the Hotel Santiago de Cuba, just off Plaza de Marte.

Cabaret

In Bayamo there's only **Cabaret Bayam**, on the *Carretera Central* just opposite the Hotel Sierra Maestra.

Holguín's equivalent of Tropicana is **Cabaret Nocturno** located about 3km (2 miles) west of town on the road to Las Tunas.

Santiago de Cuba has two major cabaret shows, **Tropicana Santiago** on the *Circunvalación* 4km (2.5 miles) northeast of Hotel Las Américas, and **Cabaret San Pedro del Mar** 7km (4.5 miles) southeast of town on the *Carretera del Morro*.

Walks & Tours

1 WESTERN CUBA

Drive

DISTANCE 345km (214 miles) **TIME** 1–2 days
START/END POINT Havana ✚ 181 E4

This appealing drive takes the traveller through the heart of Western Cuba, one of the least touristed areas of the country. It's an easy drive, quite possible in one day, though it makes sense to stay overnight at Viñales, Soroa or La Terrazas rather than heading back to Havana at sunset, especially as the road lighting at night is just about non-existent. You'll learn a lot about tobacco plantations, sample some of the local liquors, pass the time of day with lasso-wielding cowboys and enjoy grand vistas across the Gulf of Mexico. If you stay at Soroa or La Terrazas you'll also be able to relax in the verdant hill country of the Sierra del Rosario, from the bustle and traffic fumes of downtown Havana.

View across Viñales from the church bell tower
Previous page: Mule caravan by the Caribbean near Chivirico

1–2

The easiest and fastest way to drive the **Sierra del Rosario** and the north coast of Cuba is to head west along the all-but-deserted *autopista* to **Pinar del Río** (▶ 78). Once you have managed to find the

intersect, it's pretty much "plain sailing" as far as Pinar, though you should watch out for the usual stray hitchhikers, goats, cattle, abandoned vehicles and garlic salesmen.

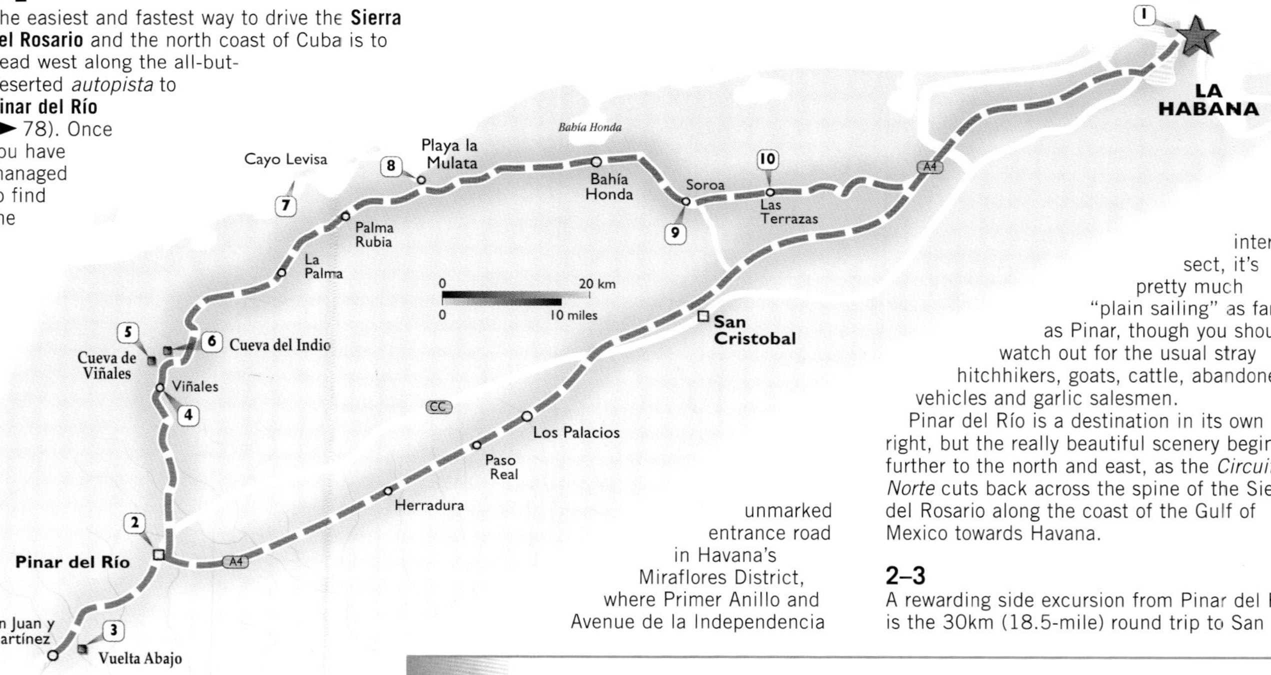

Pinar del Río is a destination in its own right, but the really beautiful scenery begins further to the north and east, as the *Circuito Norte* cuts back across the spine of the Sierra del Rosario along the coast of the Gulf of Mexico towards Havana.

2–3

A rewarding side excursion from Pinar del Río is the 30km (18.5-mile) round trip to San

unmarked entrance road in Havana's Miraflores District, where Primer Anillo and Avenue de la Independencia

LA HABANA

Las Terrazas
Soroa
Bahía Honda
Playa la Mulata
Cayo Levisa
Palma Rubia
La Palma
Cueva del Indio
Cueva de Viñales
Viñales
Bahía Honda

San Cristóbal
Los Palacios
Paso Real
Herradura

Pinar del Río
San Juan y Martínez
Vuelta Abajo

20 km
10 miles

east. You can actually see the Viñales Valley from Pinar, so it's not difficult to find. The entire northern horizon is dotted with limestone outcrops known locally as *mogotes*. Geologists explain that during the Cretaceous period around 100 million years ago underground rivers eroded the high land near present-day Viñales, creating great caves which eventually collapsed leaving the spectacular outcrops visible today.

Viñales is really just a small village, with a population of around 5,000 and a single main street. The centre of the town is **Iglesia Viñales**, a fine colonial church dating from around 1880. It's possible to climb to the top of the bell tower. From here there are good views of the entire, tobacco-rich valley. Where tobacco isn't planted, luxuriant green foliage and deep, rich red earth provide a spectacular backdrop for the numerous *mogotes*.

There's no reason to stay in Viñales, though a couple of government hotels are located in the area, the best of which is the Hotel Los Jazmines. It's a good place to stop for refreshment, however, with several restaurants and bars scattered along the main street. The whole village can be explored on foot in half an hour, and there are souvenir and art stalls in the square immediately west

Painting of tobacco farmer, on sale at Vuelta Abajo

Juan y Martínez, the small village which dominates the tobacco-growing valley of **Vuelta Abajo** (▶ 87).

3–4

Once you've finished exploring Vuelta Abajo, head back to Pinar and then north to **Viñales**, a gorgeous valley hidden away in the Sierra de los Organos which must rank among the loveliest regions of Cuba.

It's a 27km (17-mile) drive from Pinar del Río to Viñales, with a large part of the road running past the El Jíbaro Reservoir to the

of the church. If you're heading back to Havana via the *Circuito Norte* (as this drive suggests), there's a service station selling both petrol and diesel at the northeast end of the village – remember to top up!

4–5

The real joy of Viñales lies in the area of natural beauty surrounding the village known as the **Monumento Nacional de Viñales**. This comprises a series of conjoined valleys lined by towering, tree-covered *mogotes* and riddled with networks of caves. If you drive north from Viñales along the road to La Palma you'll pass several of the most interesting cave complexes. These include – 3km (1.8 miles) from Viñales – **Cueva de Viñales**, a sandstone cave which has been converted to act as a disco at night and therefore may not be to every visitor's taste.

5–6

A further 3km (1.8 miles) on the road reaches **Cueva del Indio**, a more authentic series of underground caverns reaching heights of more than 100m (328 feet) in places. It can be explored on foot for some of the way, but if you wish to see the entire complex you'll need to hire a motorboat.

6–7

Beyond Cueva del Indio the road swings northeastwards, passing **Pan de Guajaibón**, a 700m (2,296-foot) high rock tower rising straight out of the surrounding jungle. The road in this area is poor and full of potholes – watch out, too, for *guajiros* on horseback, goats, chickens, pigs and other farmyard animals, and above all for horse- or ox-drawn carts which can move extremely slowly. Shortly after the town of **La Palma** the blue waters of the Gulf of Mexico come into sight. About 30km (18.5 miles) further on a small road leads off north to the popular dive site of **Cayo Levisa**, yet another small part of the Cuban coastline associated with Ernest Hemingway, who fished for red snapper and marlin here, as well as watching for German submarines during World War II.

7–8

Just 11km (7 miles) further east, again by the shores of the Gulf of Mexico, is another reminder of Hemingway at the tiny village of **Playa la Mulata**. Here you will find a plaque informing the passer-by that "Papa" once used Cayo Paraíso, a tiny island just offshore, as a base for anti-submarine watches from his yacht *El Pilar* during the war.

8–9

After Playa la Mulata the *Circuito Norte* heads back inland, passing through the small town of **Bahía Honda** and continuing for around another 50km (31 miles) to **Mariel**, a rather shabby port town on the eastern outskirts of Havana. Unless you're really in a hurry, this route back to the capital should be avoided. Instead turn right (south) into the heart of the Sierra del Rosario at **San Diego de Núñez** (there are no signs, so ask directions about 4km/2.5 miles east of Bahía Honda). The winding mountain road leads you up to the delightful hill resort of **Soroa** (▶ 87) with excellent accommodation, good food and spectacular views. This is a first-rate place to stay the night, and in the morning – as a special indulgence – you can refresh yourself at the local waterfall.

Farmstead in the hills above Bahía Honda

Havana well before noon. Just drive south from Soroa for 7km (4.3 miles), or southeast from Las Terrazas for 8km (5 miles), and you'll be back on the *autopista* to Havana, just over an hour's comfortable drive away.

Taking a Break

Stop for lunch or refreshments at Viñales' **La Ermita** restaurant (▶ 93).

9–10

Alternatively, you may choose to turn left (east) at the small town of **Mercedita** just before Soroa and push on for 11km (7 miles) to the hill resort of **Las Terrazas**, again a fine spot to stay overnight with good food and accommodation. In the morning there's plenty of time to explore the sights around both Soroa and La Terrazas and still be back in

2 PINAR DEL RÍO
Walk

This walk guides you around Pinar del Río, the largest town in Western Cuba and an important centre of the tobacco industry. Although once obviously prosperous, Pinar del Río has fallen on hard times yet retains a faded elegance and colonial charm which are both pleasing and evocative of times past. It's not a large town – the population is currently estimated at 125,000 – and it's possible to complete the walk in around two hours. It's both pleasant and relaxing to finish the final leg by horse-drawn carriage.

The Pinar del Río *autopista* is one of the strange legacies which the communist revolution has bequeathed to Pinar del Río. Originally constructed with a view to

DISTANCE 3.5km (2 miles); suggested walk 2km (1.2 miles), horse carriage 1.5km (0.9 mile)

TIME 2–3 hours

START/END POINT Hotel Pinar del Río ✚ 180 C3

bringing this isolated western outpost into the mainstream of Cuban life, it's a six-lane highway with almost no traffic that runs straight from western Havana to the south-eastern suburbs of Pinar. There, almost without warning, it changes into the narrow main high street, Calle Martí. The drive from Havana is straightforward and takes around three hours.

Immediately to the right (north) of the *Autopista*-Martí intersection stands the four-storey Hotel Pinar del Río, built in Soviet-style in 1979 but still, probably, the best place to stay in town and also the obvious starting point for a walk around the city. It's also serves a good breakfast, which is buffet-style and included in the nightly rate.

Horse-drawn bus, Pinar del Río

0   200 metres

0   200 yards

1-2

Leave the hotel and head west up Martí, the town's main street, lined with pastel-coloured, colonnaded, single-storey buildings. After 300m (325 yards) on the left (south) side of the road you will reach the extraordinary **Museo de Ciencias Naturales**. It's not an easy building to miss, being constructed in a fantastic style incorporating neo-Gothic spires and pseudo-Moorish arches by local doctor, world traveller and enthusiastic amateur naturalist Francisco Guasch in 1914. For this reason it's also known locally as **Palacio Guasch**. Admission is US$1, which entitles you to inspect an array of taxidermy, preserved insects, and dried fish.

2-3

A further 400m (435 yards) westwards along Martí brings you to a cluster of three buildings of note centred on the Calle Martí-Isabel Rubio crossroads. The first of these is the neo-classical **Teatro José Jacinto Milanés**, a fine colonial building which has been under restoration since 1991.

3-4

Right next door is the **Museo Provincial de Historia**, Pinar del Río's main repository of its colonial past and a window on the world of the 19th century tobacco barons, though there are also a few pre-Columbian Indian artefacts. Of particular interest is the early planter's dining room complete with the original dining table.

4-5

The third building of note is the newly restored **Hotel El Globo**, which offers the usual Cuban fare and, perhaps more importantly, refreshing cold drinks – alcoholic and non-alcoholic – in a lobby bar lined with colourful Spanish tiles.

5-6

After leaving the Hotel Globo, turn south along Calle Isabel Rubio for 400m (435 yards). On the right-hand (east) side of the road you will find Pinar's most unusual institution, the **Fábrica de Bebidas Casa Garay**, a small factory – almost a cottage industry – producing two distinct versions (sweet and dry) of the famous *Guayabita del Pinar* liquor.

Fábrica de Tabacos
Francisco Donatién

⑨

Hotel Globo

⑤

⑧

Casa Natal de
Antonio Guiteras
Holmes

Catedral de
San Rosendo

⑦

Fábrica de
Bebidas
Casa Garay

⑥

GERARDO MEDINA

COLÓN

ANTONIO

MACEO

Museo
Provincial
de Historia

④

③

Teatro José
Jacinto
Milanés

RAFAEL FERRO

FRANK PAÍS

ISABEL

Museo de
Ciencias
Naturales

②

GONZÁLEZ

Hotel Pinar
del Río ①

AUTOPISTA

Distillery tours are available, as are tasting sessions and – of course – sales of this powerful alcohol, unique to Pinar del Río.

Catedral de San Rosendo

6–7

On leaving Casa Garay, backtrack about 5m (6 yards) and turn left (west) along the narrow lane which leads to Calle Gerardo Medina. Swing right (north) along the latter and you can't miss the **Catedral de San Rosendo**. The main entrance to this fine building is often closed, but visitors can generally gain access through the side entrance on weekday afternoons. All are welcome during services, with Mass held every day except Monday.

7–8

On leaving the cathedral head due west along Calle Antonio Tarafa. After just 150m (165 yards), at the junction with Calle Ormani Arenado, is the **Casa Natal de Antonio Guiteras Holmes**, a local revolutionary active during the mid-1930s.

8–9

A further 200m (220 yards) west along Calle Antonio Tarafa will bring you to Pinar del Río's second major attraction, the **Fábrica de Tabacos Francisco Donatién**, one of the best cigar factories in Cuba producing six brands

of cigar including the celebrated Vegueros brand. The factory, which employs around 200 workers, is housed in a former jail. As usual, tours are available, authorised cigars for export are for sale, and taxi-drivers waiting outside will do their best to persuade you to take the 15km (9.3 miles) drive to **Vuelta Abajo** (▶ 87), celebrated as the best cigar-producing region in Cuba. Remember to bargain – initial prices quoted are generally very inflated.

If you take this option, it will add at least two hours to your itinerary – but whether you are a cigar aficionado or a non-smoker you will learn all about cigar production and manufacture. Alternatively, walk 50m (55 yards) further west to **Plaza de la Independencia** and take a horse-drawn bus or carriage back to Hotel Pinar del Río, your original starting point.

Taking a Break

The best restaurant in town is **Rumayor** (▶ 93); for mid-walk refreshments try **Hotel El Globo** (▶ 157).

3 SIERRA DEL ESCAMBRAY

Drive

DISTANCE 87km (54 miles) or 107km (66 miles) including Playa Ancón
TIME 4–5 hours
START POINT Cienfuegos ✠ 182 B4
END POINT Trinidad or Playa Ancón ✠ 182 C3

The Sierra del Escambray is Cuba's second highest mountain range after the Sierra Maestra in Oriente, with it's highest peak – Pico San Juan, near Topes de Collantes – reaching over 1,100m (3,610 feet).

It's difficult to miss the looming crags of the Sierra del Escambray from almost anywhere in south central Cuba. Strangely serrated, saw-toothed peaks rise close to the coast between the major city of Cienfuegos and the medieval town of Trinidad, dominating the flat sugarlands which sprawl elsewhere across the landscape. They make a great excursion – one of the best drives in Cuba – and as yet are remarkably untouristed.

Cuban holiday-makers relaxing at a waterfall near Topes de Collantes

1–2
Leave Cienfuegos by the new ring road towards Jaime Gonzalez Airport and take the highway towards Cumanayagua. Just 12km (7.5 miles) beyond Caunao, and 2km (1.2 miles) before **Guaos**, watch for a non-signposted road to the left (south) and head south for 3 km (1.9 miles) to the **Jardín Botánico** (▶ 114) near the sugar mill of **Pepito Tey**. These fine gardens, entered by a long road lined with royal palms, are incredibly peaceful and secluded

2–3
From the Botanical Gardens proceed south for 11km (7 miles), passing through the town of Gordo before taking a right (east) turn to the sugar town of **Cumanayagua**. En route you will pass numerous citrus plantations, especially oranges, as well as more sugar cane than you could have imagined existed. The Sierra del

Escambray grow steadily more impressive as you proceed beyond Cumanayagua to **Manicaragua**, the latter more notable for its elaborate catholic cemetery than for its restaurants, though there are at least two small pizza and hamburger stalls on the busy main street.

3–4

Just beyond Cumanayagua, 3km (1.9 miles) east of the small village of **Barajagua**, a small (and for once signposted) road leads off south into the hills. This is a one-way excursion to **El Salto de Hanabanilla**, a small resort set high in the hills overlooking the long, narrow Hanabanilla Reservoir. If you are taking a picnic, this is as pleasant a place as any to enjoy. It's also possible to arrange fishing trips or just rent a rowing boat for an hour or two.

4–5

From Hanabanilla backtrack to Barajagua and continue east to **Manicaragua**. This is a small plains town nestling in the northern lea of the mountains – from here the climb becomes more pronounced.

5–6

From Manicaragua the road swings due south into the heart of the Sierra del Escambray via the towns of **La Piedra** and **Jibacoa**. Along the way you may see converted truck-buses full of Cubans taking a day off to bathe in one of the many waterfalls that cascade down out of the surrounding peaks. Looking back from the elevated highway at Jibacoa, there are fine views of the Hanabanilla Reservoir glinting in the sunlight far below.

This is cowboy country, and you will meet more mounted *guajiros* than trucks or buses. The road is so quiet as to be almost deserted, and if you stop the car and get out you may be overwhelmed by the powerful scent of *mariposa blanca*, a heavily-perfumed white flower which blossoms in the Sierra del Escambray and which is the national flower of Cuba.

6–7

From Jibacoa the road continues for 21km (13 miles) through winding, steep hillside covered with fern-clad trees to the settlement of **Topes de Collantes**. This hill town, billed as a health resort, stands at an altitude of 771m (2,529 feet) and is surrounded by lush forests, giant ferns and coffee plantations. It's a very popular day trip for Cubans from nearby Trinidad and for tourists from Playa Ancón. It's also about the only place between Cienfuegous and Trinidad with a half-way decent restaurant, but since Trinidad is just

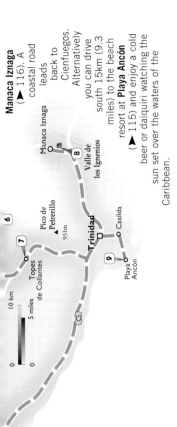

Manaca Iznaga
(▶ 116). A coastal road leads back to Cienfuegos. Alternatively you can drive south 15km (9.3 miles) to the beach resort at **Playa Ancón** (▶ 115) and enjoy a cold beer or daiquiri watching the sun set over the waters of the Caribbean.

Taking a Break
Buy a picnic lunch in Cienfuegos and eat it at **El Salto de Hanabanilla** (▶ 160).

18km (11 miles) away, you may not feel the need to bother.

7-8
It's a steep and winding road that leads down out of the Sierra del Escambray to the town of **Trinidad** (▶ 106) where you may want to stay at least one night. From here you can climb the tower of the **Museo de la Lucha Contra Bandidos** – formerly the 18th-century Convent of San Francisco de Asís.

8-9
If you arrive in Trinidad during the late afternoon and still have the energy for a little more driving, you could head east 10 km (6.2 miles) to the **Valle de los Ingenios** (▶ 115) where you can watch the sun set over the Sierra del Escambray from the tower at

Pack train of mules near Hanabanilla

4 SANTIAGO DE CUBA
Walk

DISTANCE 2.5km (1.5 miles) one way
TIME 3 hours
START POINT Plaza de Dolores ✚ 186 C3
END POINT Museo de la Lucha Clandestina ✚ 186 B4

This walk takes you through the historic heart of Santiago de Cuba, Cuba's second largest city and one of the nation's most historic and vibrant cultural centres. The walk starts in the eastern part of the city centre at Plaza de Dolores, westwards through the central part of the Old City past the Catedral de Nuestra Señora de la Asunción towards the Caribbean. This is best viewed from the *mirador* (viewpoint) of the Balcón de Velázquez towards the end of the walk.

The elegant and well shaded Plaza Dolores makes a convenient starting point for an exploration of old Santiago de Cuba, not least because several of the city's better restaurants cluster around the square and it's easy to get a cup of coffee or eat breakfast before setting off on the walk.

1–2

At the western end of Plaza de Dolores, just off Calle Aguilera on the southern side of the street stands the **Iglesia Nuestra Señora de Dolores.** Once a church of some note, this building was badly damaged by fire in the 1970s and rebuilt as a concert hall. It's a good place to watch young students of music practicing under the tutelage of their professors, with some saxophone and guitar players actually sitting in the shade on the raised steps going through their routines.

Santiago's **Catedral de Nuestra Señora de la Asunción**

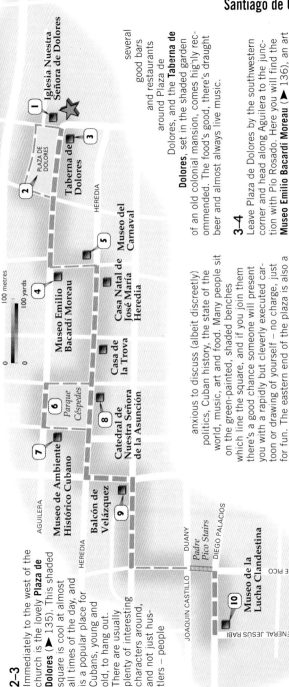

Iglesia Nuestra Señora de Dolores

PLAZA DE DOLORES

Taberna del Dolores

HEREDIA

Museo del Carnaval

Museo Emilio Bacardí Moreau

Casa Natal de José María Heredia

Casa de la Trova

Parque Céspedes

Catedral de Nuestra Señora de la Asunción

Museo de Ambiente Histórico Cubano

AGUILERA

Balcón de Velázquez

HEREDIA

JOAQUIN CASTILLO

DUANY

Padre Pico Stairs

DIEGO PALACIOS

PADRE PICO

GENERAL JESÚS RABÍ

Museo de la Lucha Clandestina

0   100 metres
0   100 yards

2–3

Immediately to the west of the church is the lovely **Plaza de Dolores** (➤ 135). This shaded square is cool at almost all times of the day, and is a popular place for Cubans, young and old, to hang out. There are usually plenty of interesting characters around, and not just hustlers – people anxious to discuss (albeit discreetly) politics, Cuban history, the state of the world, music, art and food. Many people sit on the green-painted, shaded benches which line the square, and if you join them there's a good chance someone will present you with a rapidly but cleverly executed cartoon or drawing of yourself – no charge, just for fun. The eastern end of the plaza is also a popular taxi stand, and numerous old American jalopies, lovingly cared for by their owners, can usually be seen there. There are several good bars and restaurants around Plaza de Dolores, and the **Taberna de Dolores**, set in the shaded garden of an old colonial mansion, comes highly recommended. The food's good, there's draught beer and almost always live music.

3–4

Leave Plaza de Dolores by the southwestern corner and head along Aguilera to the junction with Pío Rosado. Here you will find the **Museo Emilio Bacardí Moreau** (➤ 136), an art gallery founded in 1899 by the rum millionaire who also happened to be the first mayor of independent Santiago de Cuba. There are

View from the Balcón de Velázquez

some fine works of art and an extensive collection of weapons to be seen here, so it is well worth dropping in.

4–5

A short walk south along Pío Rosado will bring you to **Calle Heredia**, a narrow but picturesque street with two small museums, each worth a visit. The first is the small **Museo del Carnaval** (▶ 135) which provides

some idea of the wild times occurring each July, but is unfortunately a poor substitute for the real thing. Almost next door is the **Casa Natal de José María Heredia**, a Cuban poet and nationalist born here in 1803. Heredia was driven into exile by the Spanish authorities because of his nationalist views and died in Mexico in 1839.

5–6

Calle Heredia is a particularly musical street, even by Cuban standards, and Latin-Caribbean rhythms generally emanate from the nearby **Casa de la Trova**, just by the southeastern entrance to **Parque Céspedes**, the city's most important square. Parque Céspedes (▶ 134), named for the country's first independence leader, is really the heart of historic Santiago de Cuba. Immediately to the right on entering the park is the classy **Hotel Casa Granda** (▶ 146), an excellent place to stop for refreshments and to watch the goings-on in the busy square from the large, shaded first-floor bar and restaurant. At the centre of the leafy square is a bust of **Carlos Manuel de Céspedes**. Beloved and respected all over the country, he is, as a native of Oriente, particularly popular in Santiago de Cuba. To the north of the square is the very fine **Ayuntamiento** or Town Hall, which is unfortunately closed to visitors.

6–7

To the northwest of the square is the **Museo de Ambiente Histórico Cubano**, a beautifully restored colonial building also known as the **Casa de Velázquez** (▶ 134). Said to be the oldest surviving house in Santiago, it now

houses various paintings and antiques dating from the colonial period. The ground floor was once a trading house, while upstairs was the personal residence of the conquistador Diego de Velázquez.

7–8

Dominating the square from its south side is the magnificent **Catedral de Nuestra Señora de la Asunción** (➤ 134). Originally constructed in 1528, it underwent considerable restoration four centuries later and is still a splendid edifice. The remains of the famed Diego de Velázquez are said to be interred here, though nobody seems quite sure where. The building has five naves supporting a beautifully coffered ceiling and dome. Unfortunately it's often closed except during services, but the small **Museo Arquidiocesano** on the south side of the cathedral, which houses a collection of religious artefacts, furniture and paintings, is open 9 am to 5 pm weekdays and Saturday and Sunday mornings.

8–9

Leave Parque Céspedes by the southwest entrance and walk southwards along Calle Felix Peña. On the right (west) of the road, atop an old Spanish fort, is the famed **Balcón de Velázquez** where you can sip a cold drink while taking in the magnificent views across Santiago Harbour and Bay.

9–10

Continue one block further westwards and descend the flight of steps known as the **Padre Pico** stairs. From here it's a short climb west up Calle General Jesús Rabi to the **Museo de la Lucha Clandestina** (Museum of the Clandestine Struggle). Photographs and other exhibits document the struggle against the Batista dictatorship. The house at Calle General Jesús Rabi 6 is Fidel Castro's former student lodgings when a student in Santiago de Cuba. From here you can take a taxi back to Plaza de Dolores.

Taking a Break

A good place to lunch is the lobby bar over-looking Parque Céspedes at the **Hotel Casa Granda** (➤ 146). Alternatively try the excellent **Taberna de Dolores** (➤ 148) on Plaza de Dolores.

A shady break at the Taberna de Dolores

5 SIERRA MAESTRA
Drive

This is undoubtedly one of the most spectacular drives in Cuba, and well worth the effort. It is a long way, but can be halved if time is tight by starting in Marea del Portillo instead of Bayamo. Otherwise, and ideally, make it a relaxing and invigorating two day drive taking in some of the most breathtaking scenery in eastern Cuba lying between Bayamo and Santiago de Cuba, two of Oriente's most interesting cities.

DISTANCE 215km (133 miles) or 160km (99 miles)
TIME 9 hours or 4 hours
START POINT Bayamo or Marea del Portillo ⊞ 184 B2
END POINT Santiago de Cuba ⊞ 185 D2

1–2

Bayamo (▶ 130) is a delightful small town with much to see and a great place to overnight. From here, starting as early as possible, head out to the southwest of the city along the narrow but well-maintained road to **Barranca**. This is cattle country, and the sugar cane fields of central Cuba are increasingly replaced by open grazing country. From

Barranca continue west through **Veguitas** to Yara, 46km (28.5 miles) west of Bayamo.
Yara has considerable importance in Cuba's history of nationalism. It was here that Carlos Manuel de Céspedes, after freeing his slaves, fought his first battle against the Spanish in October, 1868. The town is famous for Céspedes' *Grito de Yara* or "Yara Declaration" in which he declared Cuba's independence. These events are commemorated at the

Museo Municipal, open daily except Mondays, admission US$1.

2–3

Just 40km (25 miles) south of Yara, passing through the small cattle town of Bartolomé Masó, is the **Gran Parque Nacional Sierra Maestra**, the highest mountain range in the country and famous as Fidel Castro's main redoubt in his struggle to overthrow the dictator Fulgencio Batista. Driving into the park involves climbing steep concrete access roads with strange, narrow side-tracks – these latter are used by the locals as a rapid form of transport aboard wheeled trolleys. The scenery as you climb towards Santo Domingo is spectacular, but the corrugated roads are very steep in places and not all Cuban rental cars are up to the trip. There's a fine view-point at **Balcón de la Sierra**, immediately above the Paso Malo Reservoir, then the road winds into the hills beyond **Providencia** to its ultimate destination at **Santo Domingo**.

This is as far as the drive into the Sierra Maestra goes. It's possible to trek much further, all the way to the summit of **Pico Turquino**, at 1,972m (6,468 feet) the highest

mountain in the country. However, special permits are required (obtainable at the Park Office in Santo Domingo), and you need to be really fit. The Cuban authorities remain very strict about access to these regions, which is not always allowed. The trekking fee includes a mandatory security escort.

3–4

Many people will prefer to turn round at Santo Domingo and retrace their route to Yara. From here it's a straightforward 23km (14.2-mile) drive across more cattle and sugar country to the port of **Manzanillo** (▲140). This isolated but attractive fishing harbour is a good place to take a break, especially at one of the bars along the Malecón or

A street corner in Manzanillo

The southern coast near Ocujal

Taking a Break
In Manzanillo try **Cafetería La Fuente** on Parque Céspedes; at Marea del Portillo **Hotel Farallón del Caribe** ☎ 59 4004.

seafront. The real attraction, however, is **Parque Céspedes**, Manzanillo's central square, which has some rather distinguished Andalusian-style **Moorish architecture**. The best example of this unexpected art form is the central *kiosko*, or bandstand.

4–5

From Manzanillo continue southwest by the shores of the Caribbean past the **Museo Histórico de la Demajagua**, 10km (6.2 miles) south of town, formerly the family estate of Carlos Manuel de Céspedes. It was here that the great patriot rang the bell freeing his slaves in 1868, and it remains a place of nationalist pride and pilgrimage.

5–6

The road continues southwest through Media Luna, birthplace of Celia Sánchez (▶ 62), "first lady" of the Cuban Revolution, before swinging inland after 12km (7.5 miles) to Pilón. From this point to Santiago de Cuba the highway hugs the Caribbean, sometimes so closely that your car may be covered in spray from large waves. Just east of Pilón at **Punta de Piedra** there's a good hotel and restaurant facing the turquoise Caribbean which makes a good place to stop for a meal.

If, on the other hand, you're intending an overnight stop, drive the further 7km (4.3 miles) to **Marea del Portillo** where several quality resort hotels provide comfortable accommodation and good international fare.

6–7

From Marea del Portillo the drive to **Santiago del Cuba** is pure pleasure. There's hardly any traffic, the magnificent Sierra Maestra rises sheer to your north, while the Caribbean laps or lashes at the southern side of the highway, sometimes so close that you're almost in the waves. Until fairly recently this was a very poor road, and you should watch for landslips and stray boulders. As usual in Cuba, there are no lights at all at night. You won't see

A verdant valley under the towering peaks of the Sierra Maestra

anything but buzzards, sea eagles, fishermen, goat-herds and cowboys for the remainder of the three hour drive to Santiago – though if you're lucky, at El Dian, near Ocujal, the clouds will part to reveal the towering peak of **Pico Turquino**, a splendid sight.

7–8

Beyond Pico Turqino the road continues by the Caribbean through wild country, passing the small towns of Chivirico and Caletón Blanco before skirting the **Bahía de Santiago de Cuba** and entering the city of Santiago de Cuba via its southwestern suburbs.

GETTING ADVANCE INFORMATION

Websites
- www.cubajunky.com
- www.cubatravel.cu
- www.granma.cu
- www.lahabana.com
- www.timeout.com/havana

In the UK
Cuban Ministry of Tourism
167 High Holborn
London WC1V 6PA
☎ 020 7240 6655;
fax: 020 7240 6656

In the US
There is no official Cuban
tourist representation in the
USA

BEFORE YOU GO

WHAT YOU NEED

		UK	Germany	USA	Canada	Australia	Ireland	Netherlands	Spain
● Required ○ Suggested ▲ Not required △ Not applicable	Some countries require a passport to remain valid for a minimum period (usually at least 6 months) beyond the date of entry – contact their consulate or embassy or a travel agent for details.								
Passport/National Identity Card (also check visa requirements)		●	●	●	●	●	●	●	●
Tourist Card (for holiday travel up to 4 weeks)		●	●	●	●	●	●	●	●
Onward or Return Ticket		●	●	●	●	●	●	●	●
Health Inoculations (tetanus and polio)		▲	▲	▲	▲	▲	▲	▲	▲
Health Documentation (▶ 174, Health)		△	△	△	△	△	△	△	△
Travel Insurance		○	○	○	○	○	○	○	○
Driving Licence (national) for car hire		△	△	△	△	△	△	△	△
Car Insurance Certificate (if using own car)		△	△	△	△	△	△	△	△
Car Registration Document (if using own car)		△	△	△	△	△	△	△	△

WHEN TO GO

Havana

◼ High season   ◻ Low season

JAN	FEB	MAR	APR	MAY	JUN	JUL	AUG	SEP	OCT	NOV	DEC
26°C	26°C	27°C	29°C	30°C	31°C	32°C	32°C	31°C	29°C	28°C	29°C

☀ Sun   ☁ Cloud   🌧 Wet and Windy   🌦 Sun/Showers

Cuba's subtropical climate has only two seasons, the **rainy summer** (May to October) and the relatively **dry winter** (November to April). January to April is the **sunniest time to visit**, while the **hurricane season** runs from June to November. Hurricanes are more frequent in the west of the island, particularly in Pinar del Río and Havana Provinces. Rainstorms tend to be short but heavy, and affect the central *cordillera* more than the coast. The heaviest rains are generally in September and October. Rainfall tends to be heavier in the east of the island. Because of the island's long, thin shape, few places are far from the sea and there is generally a **cooling sea breeze**. In winter it can be chilly in the higher mountains, but it's never really cold. **Humidity** ranges from the high 70s in winter to the low 80s in summer – enough to make breeze and shade attractive.

In Canada	**In Spain**	**In France**
Cuban Tourist Board	Officina de Promoción e	Office de Tourisme de Cuba
55 Queen's Street East	Información Turística de Cuba	280 Boulevard Raspail
No 705, Toronto	Paseo de la Habana 54	75014 Paris
Ontario M5H 1R5	Madrid	☎ 33 1 4538 9010;
☎ 0416 362 0700;	☎ 34 91 411 3097;	fax 33 1 4538 9930
fax: 0416 362 0702	fax 34 91 564 5804	

GETTING THERE

By Air Scheduled and charter flights operate from Britain, Continental Europe, Canada, Mexico, Jamaica and numerous other Latin American and Caribbean countries. Licensed charter flights operate from the USA (notably Miami) but **only** for those legally permitted to spend US dollars in Cuba – generally Cuban exiles. Major carriers serving Cuba include **Air Canada** (www.aircanada.ca), **Air Jamaica** (www.airjamaica.com), **Mexicana** (www.mexicana.com.mx), **British Airways** (www.britishairways.com), **Air France** (www.airfrance.com), **Air Europe** (www.easyspain.com) and the Netherlands-based **Martinair** (www.martinair.com). Most independent travellers fly into Havana's José Martí International Airport, but package tourists on "all inclusive" trips may often fly to regional airports such as Camagüey, Cienfuegos, Santiago de Cuba and Varadero. In the latter case, all local travel arrangements will have been made in advance by the responsible travel agency. There are no direct scheduled flights between the USA and Cuba.

By Sea There are **no scheduled ferry services** from neighbouring countries to Cuba. Access by private yacht or cruiser is both permitted and relatively easy.

TIME

Cuban local time is the same as Eastern Standard Time in the US, which is 5 hours behind Greenwich Mean Time (GMT -5). Clocks are turned forward an hour in late March/early April and back an hour in early October.

CURRENCY AND FOREIGN EXCHANGE

Currently three separate **currencies** circulate in Cuba. Most ordinary Cubans use the non-convertible peso or *moneda nacional* (divided into 100 centavos) theoretically equal to US$1, though the real value is nearer US4 cents. Few visitors will handle *moneda nacional*, and in any case there is little for them to buy with it. In 1994 the convertible peso, or *peso convertible*, was introduced. If you withdraw money from a Cuban ATM you will get these, and they really are exchangeable at US$1, though they must be re-exchanged before leaving the country as they are worthless outside. Virtually all tourist transactions are conducted in **US dollars**, which has effectively become the country's second currency. In tourist zones such as Varadero and Cayo Coco **euros** are also legal exchange.

Credit cards are generally only accepted at major hotels and tourist destinations in Cuba. Credit cards issued in the United States, and American Express cards wherever issued, are unusable in Cuba.

Travellers' cheques, including American Express, are accepted though those issued by US banks may be refused.

Exchange Cash and travellers' cheques can be exchanged at banks and major hotels, though it is almost impossible to change anything other than US dollars.

GMT	Cuba	USA East	Germany	Spain	Australia
12 noon	7 am	7 am	1 pm	1 pm	Sydney 10 pm

WHEN YOU ARE THERE

CLOTHING SIZES

UK	Europe	USA/Cuba	
36	46	36	**Suits**
38	48	38	
40	50	40	
42	52	42	
44	54	44	
46	56	46	
7	41	8	**Shoes**
7.5	42	8.5	
8.5	43	9.5	
9.5	44	10.5	
10.5	45	11.5	
11	46	12	
14.5	37	14.5	**Shirts**
15	38	15	
15.5	39/40	15.5	
16	41	16	
16.5	42	16.5	
17	43	17	
8	34	6	**Dresses**
10	36	8	
12	38	10	
14	40	12	
16	42	14	
18	44	16	
4.5	38	6	**Shoes**
5	38	6.5	
5.5	39	7	
6	39	7.5	
6.5	40	8	
7	41	8.5	

NATIONAL HOLIDAYS

1 Jan	Liberation Day (in 1959)
1 May	International Labour Day
26 Jul	National Rebellion Day (Assault on the Moncada Barracks in 1953)
10 Oct	Start of First War of Independence (1868)
25 Dec	Christmas Day

In addition there are unofficial holidays on 31 December, 25 July and 27 July. There are also a large number of other significant days such as the birthday of José Martí on 28 January, the Bay of Pigs Victory on 19 April, when some or all official shops and offices will close.

OPENING HOURS

○ Shops   ● Main Post Offices
● Offices   ● Attractions/Museums
● Banks   ● Pharmacies

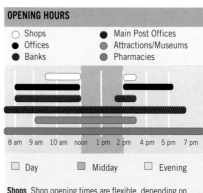

8 am   9 am   10 am   noon   1 pm   2 pm   4 pm   5 pm   7 pm

□ Day   ▨ Midday   □ Evening

Shops Shop opening times are flexible, depending on whether there's anything to sell, but dollar shops catering to tourists and dollar-wielding Cubans usually stay open longer. Generally speaking, late evening shopping is not an option.

Churches Services are generally held on Sunday morning and evening, but apart from these times, many churches remain locked.

Museums Opening and closing times vary from place to place. Bear in mind that some museums refuse entry to visitors arriving within half an hour of closing time.

POLICE 116

FIRE 115

AMBULANCE 118

PERSONAL SAFETY

• Cuba is probably the safest destination in Latin America, but in large cities and at night you should still be careful of pick-pockets and bag-snatchers. Theft of rental cars (or parts of rental cars) is also on the rise. Never leave valuables visible on the back seat.

• Personal violence against tourists is most unusual and is severely punished by the authorities.

• Women may be subject to the attentions of ultra-macho males. Avoiding direct eye contact and ignoring them is usually the best policy.

• Hustlers (*jineteros*) and prostitutes (*jineteras*) are an increasing problem. Ignoring them is usually the best policy.

Police assistance:
☎ **116** from any phone

ELECTRICITY

Cuba operates on a 110-volt AC (60 cycles) system nationwide.

Brownouts and power shortages are common. Most outlets use US-style flat, two- or three-pin plugs.

TELEPHONES

Cuba's phone system is slowly being improved, but is still generally slow and antiquated. Phone cards can be bought at all major hotels and can be used to dial abroad. Internal telephone numbers change frequently, and numbers throughout Cuba are gradually being changed to seven digits as new digital exchanges are installed. It's much cheaper to call abroad from a public call box using a phone card than from your hotel bedroom.

International Dialling Codes	
UK:	44
USA/Canada:	1
Germany:	49
Spain:	34
Netherlands:	31
Australia:	61

POST OFFICES

The postal system in Cuba is slow but usually reliable – allow six weeks for North America and perhaps longer to reach Europe. All towns have at least one post office, some several. Many gift stores and hotels sell postage-prepaid envelopes and postcards.

TIPS/GRATUITIES

Tourist hotel and restaurant charges may include a 10 per cent service charge. Elsewhere the following rates are suggested:

Restaurants	5–10%
Bars	Leave change
Taxis	Leave change
Porters	US$1
Chambermaids	US$1/day
Musicians (restaurants)	US$1

UK
☎ (7) 241771

USA
(Interests Section)
☎ (7) 344401

Canada
☎ (7) 242516

Germany
☎ (7) 332569

Spain
☎ (7) 338029

HEALTH

Insurance Medical insurance is strongly recommended, though costs for treatment are low in comparison to Europe or North America. Resorts and major cities have international clinics for tourists. Health services are high, but availability of medicines has decreased since the loss of Soviet subsidies.

Dental services Dental care should be covered by your medical insurance. Check that it is, as you will be required to pay for any treatment. Generally speaking, standards of dental care in Cuba are very high.

Weather The Caribbean sun can be extremely strong, so it's best to avoid exposure to it between 10 am and 3 pm. You can still get a good suntan in the morning and evening hours, but use a high-factor sunscreen liberally, and also wear a hat and sunglasses when moving about.

Drugs Pharmacies in Cuba are easy to find but often poorly stocked. If you require any special medication it is wise to take sufficient supplies with you. Special pharmacies, often open 24 hours a day, are available in major tourist centres, but even provincial capitals off the tourist track are poorly provisioned.

Safe Water Tap water in Cuba is not safe to drink, so make sure you have a constant supply of bottled water, available at hotels, petrol stations and many stores at reasonable prices. Ice in big hotels and resorts is quite safe to consume, but avoid it in cheap restaurants and cafés.

CONCESSIONS

Students/children Unless you are a young person actually studying in Cuba you will receive no concessions. Cuba is virtually a concession-free zone, but the price of entry to museums and other attractions is generally low.

Senior Citizens There are no special concessions for senior citizens.

TRAVELLING WITH A DISABILITY

Unfortunately, there are very few facilities for travellers with disabilities in Cuba, though a few of the major monuments have access ramps, and many resorts and hotels have wheelchair access to some rooms and most amenities. If you have special requirements, check these details carefully. Certain destinations, such as the medieval town of Trinidad, are quite unsuitable for disabled visitors.

CHILDREN

Cubans love children, and if you are travelling with them it will bring you many chance encounters with the locals. All-inclusive resorts have childcare facilities and lots of activities for kids, which makes this type of holiday so popular with families.

TOILETS

Public toilets are few and are not usually very clean. When away from your hotel discard toilet paper in the bin provided.

CUSTOMS

The import of wildlife souvenirs sourced from rare or endangered species may be either illegal or require a special permit. Before buying, check your home country's customs regulations.

GREETINGS AND COMMON WORDS

Yes/No **Sí/no**
Please **Por favor**
Thank you **Gracias**
You're welcome **De nada**
Hello **Hola**
Goodbye **Adiós**
Good morning **Buenos días**
Good afternoon **Buenas tardes**
Good night **Buenas noches**
How are you? **¿Qué tal?**
Fine, thank you **Bien, gracias**
How much is this? **¿Cuánto vale?**
I'm sorry **Lo siento**
Excuse me **Perdone**
I'd like **Me gustaría**
Open **Abierto**
Closed **Cerrado**
My name is… **Me llamo…**
What's your name? **¿Cómo se llama?**
Pleased to meet you **Mucho gusto**
My pleasure **El gusto es mío**
I'm from… **Soy de…**
Great Britain **Gran Bretaña**
England **Inglaterra**
Scotland **Escocia**
Canada **Canadá**
The United States **Los Estados Unidos**

DIRECTIONS AND TRAVELLING

I'm lost **Me he perdido**
Where is…? **¿Dónde está?**

How do I get to…? **¿Cómo se va…?**
the bank **al banco**
the post office **a la oficina de correos**
the train station **a la estación de trenes**

Where are the toilets? **¿Dónde están los servicios?**
Left **a la izquierda**
Right **a la derecha**
Straight on **todo recto**
At the corner **en la esquina**

ACCOMMODATION

Do you have a single/double room?
    ¿Le queda alguna habitación individual/doble?
with/without bath/toilet/shower
    con/sin baño/lavabo/ducha
Does that include breakfast?
    ¿Incluye desayuno?
Could I see a room? **¿Puedo ver la habitación?**
I'll take this room **Me quedo con esta habitación**
The key to the room…, please **La llave de la habitación…, por favor**
Thank you for your hospitality
    Muchas gracias por la hospitalidad

DAYS

Today **Hoy**
Tomorrow **Mañana**
Yesterday **Ayer**
Monday **Lunes**
Tuesday **Martes**
Wednesday **Miércoles**
Thursday **Jueves**
Friday **Viernes**
Saturday **Sábado**
Sunday **Domingo**

At the traffic-lights **en el semáforo**
At the crossroads **en la intersección**
Airport **Aeropuerto**
Boat **Barco**
Bus **Autobus**
Bus station **Estación/terminal**
Car **Automóvil**
Church **Iglesia**
Embassy **Embajada**
Hospital **Hospital**
Market **Mercado**
Museum **Museo**
Street **Calle**
Taxi stand **Parada de taxi**
Ticket **Boleto**

NUMBERS

0 **cero**	10 **diez**	20 **veinte**	200 **doscientos**
1 **uno**	11 **once**	21 **veintiuno**	300 **trescientos**
2 **dos**	12 **doce**	30 **treinta**	400 **cuatrocien-**
3 **tres**	13 **trece**	40 **cuarenta**	**tos**
4 **cuatro**	14 **catorce**	50 **cincuenta**	500 **quinientos**
5 **cinco**	15 **quince**	60 **sesenta**	600 **seiscientos**
6 **seis**	16 **dieciséis**	70 **setenta**	700 **setecientos**
7 **siete**	17 **diecisiete**	80 **ochenta**	800 **ochocientos**
8 **ocho**	18 **dieciocho**	90 **noventa**	900 **novecientos**
9 **nueve**	19 **diecinueve**	100 **cien**	1000 **mil**

Useful words and phrases 175

RESTAURANT

I'd like to book a table **¿Me gustaría reservar una mesa?**

A table for **Una mesa para**

Have you got a table for two, please? **¿Tienen una mesa para dos personas, por favor?**

Could we see the menu, please? **¿Nos podría traer la carta, por favor?**

Could I have the bill, please? **¿La cuenta, por favor?**

service charge includued **servicio incluido**

breakfast **el desayuno**

lunch **el almuerzo**

dinner **la cena**

table **una mesa**

waiter/waitress **camarero/camarera**

starters **los entremeses**

main course **el plato principal**

dessert **postres**

bill **la cuenta**

MENU READER

a elegir of your choice

a la brasa braised

a la parilla grilled

al carbon barbecued

al horno baked

al mojo de ajo in butter and garlic

al vapor steamed

aceituna olive

agua water

aguacate avocado

ajo garlic

arroz rice

asado roasted

atún tuna

azúcar sugar

bacalao cod

bebida drink

bistec steak

bocadillo sandwich

boniato sweet potato

café coffee

caldo soup

camarones shrimp

cangrejo crab

carne meat

cebolla onion

cerdo pork

cerveza beer

champiñones mushroom

chorizo spicy sausage

chuleta chop

cocido stew

cocina kitchen

coco coconut

condimentado (-a) spicy

congrí rice with red beans

cordero lamb

cortado (-a) en cubos diced

crudo rare

dulce sweet

ejotes green (French) beans

empanado (-a) breaded

en escabeche marinated

ensalada salad

entremés hors d'oeurve

especialidades de la casa house specialities

especialidades locales local specialities

fideos noodles

filete fillet steak

fricasé meat stew

frijoles beans

fritas fries or chips

frito fried

fruta fruit

gaseosas sodas, carbonated drinks

guayaba guava

hamburguesa hamburger

helado ice cream

hervido boiled

hielo ice

huevo egg

huevos fritos/revueltos fried/scrambled eggs

jamón ham

jugo de fruta fruit juice

langosta lobster

leche milk

lechuga lettuce

legumbres vegetables

limón lemon

maíz corn

malanga taro

mantequilla butter

manzana apple

mariscos seafood

mermelada jam

moros y cristianos rice with black beans

mortadela sausage

naranja orange

paella seafood and rice casserole

pan bread

patatas potato

pepino cucumber

pescado fish

picadillo beef hash

pimienta pepper

piña pineapple

plátano banana

pollo chicken

puerco pork

queso cheese

res beef

ron rum

rosbif roast beef

sal salt

salchicha sausage

salsa sauce

sopa soup

tasajo salt-dried beef

té tea

ternera veal

tocino bacon

tomate tomato

tortilla omelette

tostada toasted

tostones banana chips

vegetariano vegetarian

vino wine

zanahoria carrot

IF YOU NEED HELP

Help! **¡Socorro! / ¡Ayuda!**

Could you help me, please? **¿Podría ayudarme, por favor?**

Do you speak English? **¿Habla ingles?**

I don't understand **No comprendo**

I don't speak Spanish **No hablo español**

Could you call a doctor? **¿Podría llamar a un medico, por favor?**

Atlas

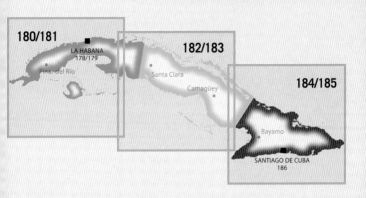

180/181

LA HABANA
178/179

Pinar del Río

182/183

Santa Clara

Camagüey

184/185

Bayamo

SANTIAGO DE CUBA
186

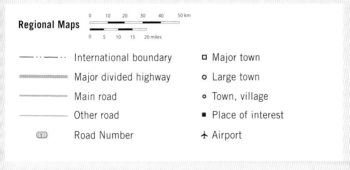

Regional Maps

0   10   20   30   40   50 km

0   5   10   15   20 miles

—·—··—·· International boundary

▭ Major town

Major divided highway

○ Large town

Main road

○ Town, village

Other road

■ Place of interest

⬭ Road Number

✈ Airport

City Plan

La Habana

0   300 metres

0   300 yards

Santiago de Cuba

0   300 metres

0   300 yards

Main road

▨ Important building

Other road

▧ Park

}·········{ Tunnel

◪ Featured place of interest

⁵ La Habana

MALECÓN

MALECÓN

LINEA

Malecón

LINEA

AVENIDA DE LOS PRESIDENTES

23 (RAMPA)

HUMBOLDT

HOSPITAL

ESPADA

VAPOR

CALZADA DE INFANTA

27 DE NOVIEMBRE

SAN LÁZARO

HAMEL

SOLEDAD

ARAMBURU

LINEA

VEDADO

CONCORDIA

SAN FRANCISCO

HOSPITAL

NEP

SAN MIGUEL

PASEO

SANTA FE

ESPADA

SAN RAFAEL

SAN MARTÍN

RONDA

VALLE

ZANJA

SALUD

Parque
John Lennon

ZAPATA

JESÚS PEREGRIN

PÓCITO

AVENIDA SALVADOR

23 (RAMPA)

ENRIQUE V

XIFRE

SITIOS

PLASENCIA

MALOJA

RETIRO

CALZADA DE INFANTA

CALZADA DE ZAPATA

AVENIDA RANCHO BOYEROS

LUGAREÑO

POZOS DULCES

BRUZON

ALMENDARES

35

19 DE MAYO

AVENIDA CARLOS M. DE CÉSPEDES

AMEZAGA

P. LACOSTE

PERERA

SAN MARTÍN

33

PASEO

SUÁREZ

TERRITORIAL

AVENIDA 20 DE MAYO

AMENIDAD

Cementerio de Colón

37

PANCHITO GÓMEZ

MASON

GRAL E NÚÑEZ

PEDRO

NUEVA

AVENIDA DE COLÓN

ERMITA

CLAVEL

SAN PABLO

AUDITOR

PEDRO PEREZ

PATRIA

AVENIDA DE LA INDEPENDENCIA

MARINO

BELLAVISTA

PANORAMA

HIDALGO

ESTANCIA

LOMBILLO

SAN PEDRO

CALZADA DE AYESTARÁN

MARIANO

DOMÍNGUEZ

SAN PEDRO

SARAVIA

LOMA

ZEQ

TULIPÁN

LA ROSA

PIÑERA

LOMBILLO

CONILL

OESTE

ESTE

FACTOR

ESTANCIA

AYUNTAMIENTO

VISTA HERMOSA

FALGUERAS

SANTA CATALINA

CALZADA DEL CERRO

SANTA ANA

NUEVO
VEDADO

SANTA ANA

ERMITA

SANTA ANA

SANTOS
SUAREZ

SANTA ANA

CARMEN

FERRER

SAN ELIAS

ST. TERESA

ZARAGOZA

PEÑON

CERRO

DUREGE

CALZADA DE BUENOS AIRES

CALZADA DE PUENTES GRANDES

MANILA

SAN CRISTOBAL

CAÑONGO

GABRIEL

ULLOA

RECURSO

REPARTO

GENIOS

PRIMELLES

CHURRUCA

ATOCHA

SANTO TOMAS

SAN SALVADOR

SUARTE

MAGNOLIA

FLORENCIA

SAN ANSELMO

SANTA MARIA

SANTA ROSA

CADIZ

PRENSA

COLON

INFANTA

REYES

SAN CARLOS

PARQUE

MACEDONIA

CEREZO

VIA

CALZADA DE PUENTES GRANDES

VELARDE

SALVADOR

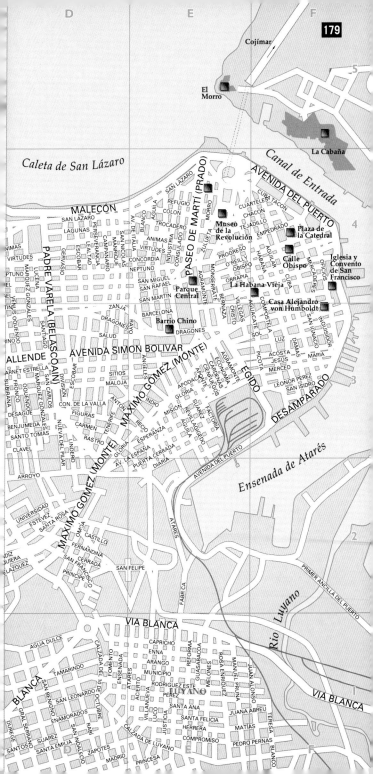

Cojímar

D E F

El Morro

La Cabaña

Caleta de San Lázaro

Canal de Entrada

AVENIDA DEL PUERTO

MALECÓN

SAN LÁZARO

LAGUNAS

ANIMAS

VIRTUES

PERSEVERANCIA
LEALTAD
ESCOBAR
GERVASIO

SAN NICOLÁS
MANRIQUE
CAMPANARIO

AV. DE ITALIA

BLANCO
TROCADERO
COLON
REFUGIO

SAN LÁZARO
AGUILA

ANIMAS
VIRTUES
CONCORDIA
NEPTUNO

INDUSTRIA
CONSULADO

MONSERRATE

PASEO DE MARTI (PRADO)

ZULUETA
MORRO

CUBA
TACON
CUARTELES

CHACON
TEJADILLO
EMPEDRADO

Museo
de la
Revolución

Plaza de
la Catedral

PADRE VARELA (BELASCOAIN)

GERVASIO
ESCOBAR
LEALTAD
LUCENA

MARQUES GONZALEZ

OQUENDO

NEPTUNO

SAN MIGUEL
SAN RAFAEL
SAN MARTIN

ZANJA

AGRAMONTE

PROGRESO
O'REILLY
OBISPO
OBRAPIA

AGUACATE
COMPOSTELA

AGUIAR
HABANA

CUBA

MERCADERES
OFICIOS

Calle
Obispo

Iglesia y
Convento
de San
Francisco

Parque
Central

BERNAZA
VILLEGAS
CRISTO

La Habana Vieja

Casa Alejandro
von Humboldt

SAN IGNACIO
INQUISIDOR

ALLENDE

AVENIDA SIMON BOLIVAR

DRAGONES
RAYO
SALUD

BARCELONA

Barrio Chino

DRAGONES

ANGELES

LUZ
ACOSTA
JESÚS
MERCED

SOL
PICOTA
DAMAS

EGIDO

DESAMPARADO

DIVISIÓN

ESCOBAR

SAN CARLOS
MARQUES GONZALEZ
OQUENDO

SITIOS
MALOJA

INDIO

ANTON RECIO
TENERIFE

MISION
ESPERANZA

APODACA
GLORIA

CIENFUEGOS
CARDENAS
ECONOMIA
ARSENAL

SUAREZ
REVILLAGIGEDO
AGUILA

FACTORIA

LEONOR PEREZ
SAN ISIDRO

MÁXIMO GOMEZ (MONTE)

ARNET ESTRELLA

ESTRELLA
FRONCO
DESAGUE
BENJUMEDA
SANTO TOMÁS
CLAVEL

CON. DE LA VALLA
FIGURAS
CARMEN
RASTRO

GLORIA

ÁV. LA ESPAÑA
PUERTA CERRADA
DIARIA

NUEVA DEL PILAR
INDIO

ARROYO

AVENIDA DEL PUERTO

Ensenada de Atarés

UNIVERSIDAD
ESTEVEZ
SANTA ROSA

OMOA
CASTILLO

FERNANDINA
CERRADA
SAN FRANCISCO
PRINCIPE

SAN FELIPE

ATARÉS

MÁXIMO GOMEZ (MONTE)

DIZ
QUERA
ELAZQUEZ

FABRICA

PRIMER ANCILLA DEL PUERTO

Rio Luyano

BLANCA

VIA BLANCA

AGUA DULCE

CALZADA DE 10 DE OCTUBRE
TAMARINDO

SAN BENIGNO
SAN LEONARDO
ENAMORADOS
RABI

CAPRICHO
ENNA
ARANGO
FOMENTO
ENSENADA
ATARÉS
ACERO
MUNICIPIO

REFORMA
GUASABACOA
MELONES

ROSA ENRIQUEZ

MANUEL PRUNA

JUAN ALONSO

VIA BLANCA

BLANCA

GRAL SERRANO
SUAREZ
SANTOS
SANTA EMILIA

ZAPOTES
MADRID
PRINCESA

RODRIGUEZ ESTE
PEREZ

SANTA ANA
SANTA FELICIA
HERRERA
COMPROMISO

LUYANO

VILLANUEVA
LUCO
JUSTICIA

CALZADA DE LUYANO

JUANA ABREU

MATÍAS

PEDRO PERNAS

TERESA
BLANCO

D E F

GRAL SERRANO
SAN INDALECIO

5

4

3

2

1

A   B   C

Golfo de Guanahacabibes

Mar Caribe

Los Morros

La Bajada
El Cayuco
Valle San Juan
Las Martinas

Bahía de Corrientes

Bahía de Guadiana

Ciudad Bolívar
Sandino
La Fé
Cortés

Bahía de Cortés

Ensenada de Coloma

Cayos de San Felipe

Cayos Los Indios

Cabo Francés

Caleta Grande

Arroyos de Mantua

Mantua
La Manigua
Guane
San Juan y Martínez
San Luis
El Rosario
La Coloma
Punta de Cartas

Vuelta Abajo
Pinar del Río

R. Mantua

591m
323m

Cayo Rapado Grande
Cayo de Buena Vista

Dimas

Ensenada de Dimas

Minas de Matahambre

Bahía Santa Lucía

Cayo Jutías

Santa Lucía

San Cayetano
Puerto Esperanza
El Rosario

Manuel Sanguily

Playa la Mulata
Bahía de la Mulata
Playa el Morillo
Playa Carnero

Harlem
Blanca Arena
Bahía de Honda

San Vicente
Pan de Azúcar
Viñales
Hoyo la Mar

La Palma
523m
San Andrés

699m
655m

San Diego de los Baños
Los Pala
Paso Real
Herradura
Consolación del Sur
El Moncada

Z

Boca de San Diego
Pinar
Playa Daya
Playa el Guanal

R. Hondo

A4

Estrecho de la Florida

Bahía de la Habana · Cojímar · Alamar · Santa María del Mar · Guanabo · Boca de Jaruco · Santa Cruz Del Norte · Arcos de Canasí · Bahía de Matanzas

LA HABANA

Augusto César Sandino · Quiebra Hacha · Bahía de Cabañas · Playa Baracoa · Santa Fe · Mosquito · La Boca · Mariel · Bauta · Caimito · San Miguel · Jaruco · Carboneras · **MATANZAS**

Cabañas · San Claudio · Museo Hemingway · Casiguas · Aguacate · Coliseo · Máx

Bahía Honda · Las Terrazas · **San Antonio de los Baños** · Parque Lenin · Madruga · Jovellano

Soroa · **Artemisa** · **Güira de Melena** · **San José de las Lajas** · Palos · Güira de M

San Cristobal · Candelaria · Camacho · Batabanó · Melena del Sur · Vegas · Bolondrón · Agram

Los Pinos · El · Playa · Playa · Playa · Playa del Caimito · El Estante

José · Corojal · Majana · Guanimar · Playa del Cajío · Rosario · R. Negro

Martí · San Juan de Marcos

Zumalacarry · Cayos los Guzmanes · Cayo Mal País · Ensenada de la Broa

Santa Rosa · Ensenada de Dayaniguas · Aus

ar de la Catalina · Maneadero · Santo Tomás

ayaniguas · Cayo Monterrey · **PENÍNSULA DE ZAPATA**

Cayos Del Hombre · Golfo de Batabano · Cayo Gordas · Buena Ventura

Islas de Mangles · Cayo del Macío · La Salina

Nueva Gerona · Chacón · Playa Bibijagua · Cayo el Navío · Cayo Diego Pérez · Cayos Blancos

La Demajagua · Cayo Triángulo · Cayo Guayabo

Atanagildo Cajigal · Cayo Balandras

La Fé · Argelia Libre · La Reforma · Cayo San Juan

La Victoria · iguanea · Cayo Rabihorcados

Cayo Piedra · Cayo Matías · Cayo el Rosario

Cayo Cantiles

Rincón Del Guanal

Archipiélago de los Canarreos

182

181

Canal de San Nicolas

Cayo Cruz del Padre
Cayos de las
Cinco Leguas
Cayos Juan Clarito
Cayos Falcones
Cayo Blanquizal
*Bahía de
Cárdenas*
Varadero
Cárdenas
La Teja
Bahía de Santa Clara
Hoyo Colorado
Martí
Itabo
Corralillo
Cayo las Picuas
Cayos Dromedarios
Máximo Gómez
seo
Isabela de Sagus
*Bahía de
Uvero*
Cayo la Vaca
Jovellanos
Julio Reyes
Cairo
Guillermo Llabre
Guamutas
Rancho Velóz
Quintín Banderas
Playa Uvero
Playa Piñón
Güira de Macurijes
Sergio Gonzáles
Los Arabos
Sagua la Grande
*Ensenada de
Cayo Vaca*
Emilio Córdova
El Santo
Agramonte
Colón
R. Palmillas
San Pedro
De Mayabón
Casajal
Rodrigo
Cifuentes
Viana
Camacho
san Juan
de Marcos
Reynold García
Manguito
Manacas
Mata
Encrucijada
Jaguey
Grande
Jesús Rabi
Aluja
Santo Domingo
Jícotea
Hatillo
Australia
Amarillas
La Piragua
Esperanza
Remedios
o Tomás
Zarabanda
Cartagena
Lajas
Ranchuelo
SANTA CLARA
Playa Larga
Aguada de
Pasajeros
Arriete-Ciego Montero
Falcón
Placetas
Ventura
Antonio Sánchez
Abreus
Ariza
Espartaco
Jorobada
General Carillo
Guillermo Moncada
Palmira
Matagua
Jar
Cayo Ramona
CIENFUEGOS
La
Macagua
La
Moza
Manicaragua
Agabama
Jiqui
ina
Juraguá
Pepito
Tey
Ciro
Redondo
Fomento
Playa Girón
Castillo de Jagua
Arímao
*Presa del
Hanabanilla*
Tuinucú
Ca
Biancos
La Sierrita
Sancti Spíritus
Bahía de Cochinos
Topes de Collantes
931m
1140m
Valle de
los Ingenios
842m
Banao
Trinidad
Casilda
San Pedro
Pojabo
Playa Ancón
Mapos
*Ensenada de
Casilda*

181

Cayo
Bal as

Mar Caribe

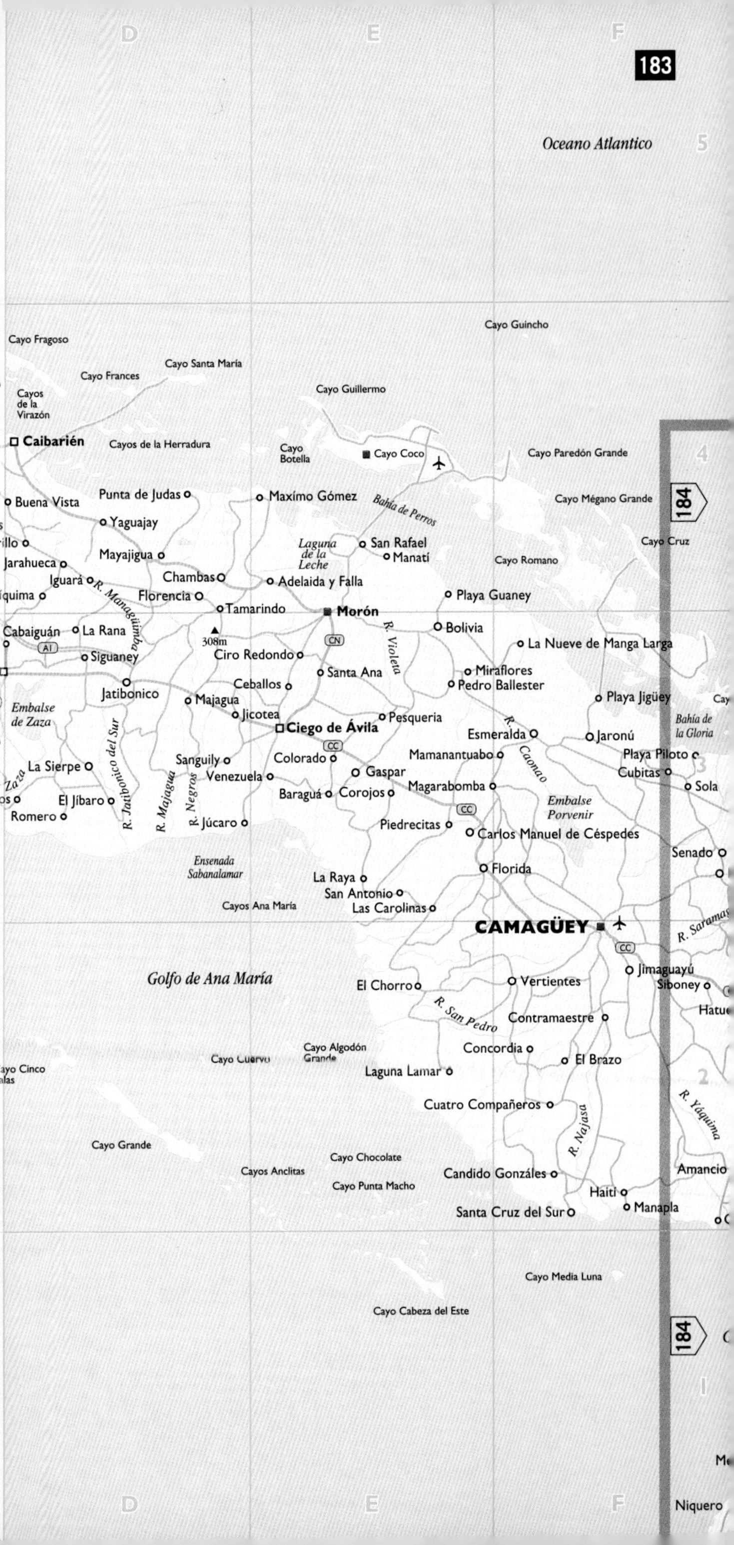

Oceano Atlantico

5

Cayo Guincho

Cayo Fragoso

Cayo Santa María

Cayo Frances

Cayo Guillermo

Cayos
de la
Virazón

□ Caibarién   Cayos de la Herradura

Cayo
Botella   ■ Cayo Coco ✈   Cayo Paredón Grande

4

184

o Buena Vista   Punta de Judas o   o Maximo Gómez   Bahía de Perros   Cayo Mégano Grande

Cayo Cruz

s   o Yaguajay   Cayo Romano

illo o   Mayajigua o   Laguna
de la
Leche   o San Rafael   o Manatí

Jarahueca o   o Iguará   R. Mangarimba   Chambas O   o Adelaida y Falla

íquima o   Florencia o   o Tamarindo   ■ Morón   o Playa Guaney

Cabaiguán   o La Rana   308m   R. Violeta   o Bolivia   o La Nueve de Manga Larga

o   A1   o Siguaney   Ciro Redondo o   (CN)

Embalse   o Jatibonico   Ceballos o   o Santa Ana   o Miraflores   o Playa Jigüey   Cay
de Zaza   o Majagua   o Jicotea   □ Ciego de Ávila   o Pesquería   o Pedro Ballester   Bahía de
la Gloria

R. Jatibonico del Sur   Sanguily o   Colorado o   (CC)   Esmeralda o   R. Caonao   o Jaronú   Playa Piloto o

La Sierpe o   Venezuela o   o Gaspar   Mamanantuabo o   Cubitas o   o Sola

os o   El Jíbaro   R. Negros   Baraguá o   o Corojos   Magarabomba o

Romero o   R. Júcaro o   (CC)   Embalse
Porvenir

Piedrecitas o   o Carlos Manuel de Céspedes   Senado o

o

Ensenada
Sabanalamar   La Raya o   o Florida

San Antonio o

Cayos Ana María   Las Carolinas o   CAMAGÜEY ■ ✈

R. Saram

(CC)

Golfo de Ana María   El Chorro o   o Vertientes   o Jimaguayú

Siboney o

Contramaestre o   Hatue

Cayo Cuervo   Cayo Algodón
Grande   Concordia o   o El Brazo   R. Yáquima

Cayo Cinco
Balas   Laguna Lamar o   2

Cuatro Compañeros o   R. Najasa

Cayo Grande   Amancio

Cayo Chocolate   Candido Gonzáles o   o

Cayos Anclitas   Cayo Punta Macho   Haiti o

Santa Cruz del Sur o   o Manapla   o C

Cayo Media Luna

Cayo Cabeza del Este   184

C

l

Me

D   E   F   Niquero

5

Canal Viejo de Bahama

Cayo Guajaba

Bahía de la Gloria

ruz

to○

Sola

Cayo Sabinal

Punta de Prácticos

Ensenada de Sabinal

Senado○ ○Lugareño ○Nuevitas

Minas Bahía de Nuevitas

Crucero de Lugareño Playa la Victoria

Bahía de Nuevas Grandes

Bahía de Manatí

Playa Uvero

Bahía de Malagueta

Bahía de Puerto Padre

Bahía de Gibara

R. Saramaguacán

Jucaral○ Camalote ○Puerto Manatí

ayú
oney○ Sibanicú Manatí

Hatuey○ Cascorro Playa la Jibara Puerto Padre ○Lora

Martí○ Vázquez○ ○San Manuel

R. Las Piedras R. Las Cabreras R. Manzanillo R. Manatí

Gibara■ Guardalavaca

Palo Seco Velasco

R. Yáquima Guáimaro ○Bartle San Andrés○ Santa Luc

Colombia○ Jobabo □Las Tunas Melones

Calixto Buenaventura HOLGUÍN■ Tacajó

R. Jobabo R. Tana R. Sevilla R. Hormiguero

Amancio○ Omaja○ ○Mir Báguano

Sábalo○ ○Dormitorio Antonio Maceo Cristino Naranjo○ R. Mejías

a Guayabal○ Playa Habenero Cueto○ R. Centeno

Cayos de Sevilla Vado del Yeso R. Salada San German○

Ensenada Birama R. Cauto ○Guamo Alto Cedro ○Bir

Henequén○ ○Río Cauto Mangos de Baragúa○

Golfo de Guacanayabo R. Buey BAYAMO✈ Jiguaní○ Ju

R. Cauto Pal

Manzanillo■ Veguitas○ ○Barranca Santa Rita○ Contramaestre○

San Francisco○ ○Yara ○Guisa Palma Soriano□ C

Campechuela○ ○Israel Licea Bueyito○ AI

Media Luna○ ○San Ramón Caney de las Bartolomé Buey ○Guamá

Mercedes Masó Arriba Victorino○ 595m▲ El Cobre■

Niq○ero Aguacate 1128m▲

R. Callejón R. Bayonita 1097m▲ Castillo de

La Marea ○San Lorenzo Santo Domingo San Pedro del Morro

Belíc La Güira La Plata 1972m▲ ○Ocujal Uvero○ Chivirico○

Pilón○ Marea del Portillo Bahía de Santia

○Cabo Cruz

Ensenada de Mora

Mar Caribe

183

A B C

I

5

Oceano Atlantico

4

3

o Guayacanes

Lucía   o Los Angeles

Banes o
o Embarcadero de Banes
Bahía de Banes

ajó   o Antilla
o Deleite   o El Ramón
Guatemala o   o Carbonera

Bahía de Levisa

Bahía Sagua de Tánamo

o Nicaro
Mayari o   o Levisa   o Cayo Mambí   o Moa   Cayo Moa Grande
o Sagua de Tánamo   o Punta Gorda

R. Mayarí   R. Levisa   1231m ▲   1175m ▲

Birán   San Juan o   R. Sagua
995m ▲   o Mayarí Arriba
o Julio A. Mella   o La Caridad   o Palenque   *Bahía de Miel*
Palmarito de Cauto   La Jaiba o   o Bernardo   R. Duaba   ■ Baracoa
o Chile   o La Prueba   Bayate o   862m ▲   Jamal o   o Mesa Abajo
719m ▲   R. Cuba   R. Sabanalum   725m ▲   R. Maya   Maisí
o Dos Caminos   El Salvador o   1059m ▲   R. Jojo   o La Máquina
o La Maya   A1   747m ▲   o Jamaica   1176m ▲   CC   o Cojobabo
SANTIAGO   CC   Imías o
DE CUBA   Niceto Pérez o   GUANTÁNAMO
de   o La Gran Piedra   Caimanera o   o Mártires de la Frontera   o San
iro   Parque ■   Antonio del Sur
rro   Baconao   ■ Comunidad   o Playa Uvero
Artística Verraco   *Bahía de Guantánamo*

antiago de Cuba

I

Santiago de Cuba

Bahía de
Santiago
de Cuba

Terminal
Mambisa

Streets and avenues

AVE DE LOS LIBERTADORES
AVENIDA GARZÓN
ZAMORANA
12 DE AGOSTO
AVENIDA JESÚS MENÉNDEZ
PASEO DE MARTÍ
JOSÉ A. SACO
CALLE 2
CALLE J
CALLE H
CALLE G
CALLE G
CALLE D
CALLE G
CALLE B
CALLE A
CALLE A
ANGEL GUERRA
CARLOS APONTE
JUAN C. ZENEA
JOSÉ A. SACO
B. BETANCOURT
P. MARTÍNEZ
FÉLIX VARELA
HEREDIA
PRIMERA
SEGUNDA
TERCERA
GENERAL CARLOS ROLOFF
GRAL. FRANCISCO PÉ
GENERAL
SERAFÍN
G MONCADA
GENERAL PORTUONDO
SATURNINO LORA
BARNADA
BARNADA
DONATO MÁRMOL
LOS MACEO
MAYÍA RODRÍGUEZ
NARCISO LÓPEZ
SAO DEL INDIO
SAN BARTOLOMÉ
HARTMAN
GENERAL LACRET
FÉLIX PEÑA
SAN FERMÍN
GONZALO DE QUESADA
NARCISO LÓPEZ
SAO DEL INDIO
LOS MACEO
M. DELGADO
10 DE OCTUBRE
SÁNCHEZ HECHAVARRÍA
PERALEJO
JOBITO
F. FUENTES
MÁXIMO GÓMEZ
MÁXIMO GÓMEZ
MÁXIMO GÓMEZ
J. M. GÓMEZ
PÍO ROSADO
GENERAL PORTUONDO
P. VALIENTE
JUAN BAUTISTA SAGARRA
SÁNCHEZ HECHAVARRÍA
SAN AUGUSTÍN
BAYAMO
AGUILERA
MAYÍA RODRÍGUEZ
HEREDIA
PADRE QUIROGA
BARTOLOMÉ MASÓ
PADRE PICO
CORNELIO ROBÉN
AGUILERA
HEREDIA
BARTOLOMÉ MASÓ
J. C. DUANY
DIEGO PALACIOS
JOSÉ A. SACO
NTE
AL LACRET
X PEÑA
MAN
ADO

Points of interest

Iglesia Nuestra
Señora de Dolores
Taberna de
Dolores
Plaza de
Dolores
Museo del
Carnaval
Museo Emilio
Bacardí Moreau
Casa Natal de
José María
Heredia
Museo del Ron
Casa de
la Trova
Museo de Ambiente
Histórico Cubano
Catedral de Nuestra
Señora de la
Asunción
Balcón de
Velázquez
Padre
Pico Stairs

Picture credits

The Automobile Association wishes to thank the following photographers and libraries for their assistance in the preparation of this book:

Front cover, back cover and spine: AA World Travel Library/Clive Sawyer

COLUMBIA/COURTESY KOBAL COLLECTION 25c, 25tl; CORBIS 16/17 (Arne Hodalic), 16b (Robert van der Hilst), 18 (Bettmann); MARY EVANS PICTURE LIBRARY 14t, 20/21, 23c; HULTON ARCHIVE/GETTY IMAGES 15b, 24b, 26c.

All remaining pictures are held in the Association's own library (AA PHOTOLIBRARY) and were taken by DAVID HENLEY with the exception of the following: CLIVE SAWYER 6/7, 7t, 8tl, 10t, 10b, 11t, 11r, 20b, 23b, 24/5, 27, 30tl, 101t.

Abbreviations for terms appearing above: (t) top; (b) bottom; (l) left; (r) right; (c) centre.

Questionnaire

SPIRAL GUIDE

Dear Traveller
Your comments, opinions and recommendations are very important to us. So please help us to improve our travel guides by taking a few minutes to complete this simple questionnaire.

You do not need a stamp (unless posted outside the UK). If you do not want to remove this page from your guide, then photocopy it or write your answers on a plain sheet of paper.

Send to: **The Editor, Spiral Guides, AA World Travel Guides, FREEPOST SCE 4598, Basingstoke RG21 4GY.**

Your recommendations...
We always encourage readers' recommendations for restaurants, night-life or shopping – if your recommendation is used in the next edition of the guide, we will send you a FREE AA Spiral Guide of your choice. Please state below the establishment name, location and your reasons for recommending it.

_____

_____

_____

_____

_____

Please send me AA Spiral _____
(see list of titles inside the back cover)

About this guide...
Which title did you buy?

_____ **AA Spiral**

Where did you buy it? _____

When? m m / y y

Why did you choose an AA Spiral Guide? _____

_____

_____

_____

Did this guide meet your expectations?

Exceeded ☐   Met all ☐   Met most ☐   Fell below ☐

Please give your reasons _____

_____

_____

_____

_____

continued on next page...

Were there any aspects of this guide that you particulanly liked?

_____

_____

_____

_____

_____

Is there anything we could have done better?

_____

_____

_____

_____

About you...

Name (Mr/Mrs/Ms) _____

Address _____

_____

_____ Postcode _____

Daytime tel no _____ email _____

Please _only_ give us your email address and mobile phone number if you wish to hear from us about other products and services from the AA and partners by email or text or mms.

Which age group are you in?

Under 25 ☐   25–34 ☐   35–44 ☐   45–54 ☐   55–64 ☐   65+ ☐

How many trips do you make a year?

Less than one ☐   One ☐   Two ☐   Three or more ☐

Are you an AA member? Yes ☐   No ☐

About your trip...

When did you book? mm / y y   When did you travel? mm / y y

How long did you stay? _____

Was it for business or leisure? _____

Did you buy any other travel guides for your trip? ☐ Yes   ☐ No

If yes, which ones? _____

_____

Thank you for taking the time to complete this questionnaire. Please send it to us as soon as possible, and remember, you do not need a stamp (unless posted outside the UK).

The information we hold about you will be used to provide the products and services requested and for identification, account administration, analysis, and fraud/loss prevention purposes. More details about how that information is used is in our privacy statement, which you'll find under the heading "Personal Information" in our terms and conditions and on our website: www.theAA.com. Copies are also available from us by post, by contacting the Data Protection Manager at AA, Southwood East, Apollo Rise, Farnborough, Hampshire GU14 0JW

We may want to contact you about other products and services provided by us, or our partners (by mail, telephone) but please tick the box if you DO NOT wish to hear about such products and services from us by mail or telephone. ☐